COVID, College,
&
Life Transitions

B J   B A R N E S

Fulton Books, Inc.
Meadville, PA

Published by Fulton Books 2021

ISBN 978-1-63710-732-4 (paperback)
ISBN 978-1-63860-700-7 (hardcover)
ISBN 978-1-63710-731-7 (digital)

Printed in the United States of America

Author's Notes

The people, places, and names you see in this book have all, at one point or another, touched me dearly and have all played a significant role in my coming-of-age journey. While I have replaced a majority of them with pseudonyms to protect their privacy, I can assure you they are all, in fact, real. On another note, no matter how outrageous, unbelievable, or straight-up insane these stories may seem, I can also assure you they are, in fact, true accounts of events that have unfolded within my adolescent years. These essays were written with the full intent to provide every senior of the class of 2020 their just closure and to extend the advice learned firsthand to every graduating class that comes after. If I could have one wish pertaining to the contents inside, it would be that they supply closure to those who went through what I did and to provide wisdom and foresight to those who haven't. May you laugh, cry, and above all resonate with the experiences that I am about to share.

Preface

After experiencing changes—some drastic and others not so much—I've come to terms with the reality that is moving forward. Moving forward while paying respects to what brought me here. This past year was home to people, places, and moments that ultimately define who I am. It is also home to some of the loneliest points in my life. Within the last year, I have graduated high school and started anew at college. I have discovered the inevitable revelation that is so commonly known as one's first broken heart. I've experienced firsthand what it is like to be on top of the world only to have it prematurely dismantled right before my very eyes. I made foolish decisions that only came back to ridicule me all the same. Oh, and I was lucky enough to survive a global pandemic, but perhaps most of all, this last year, I was caught between a doorway. A doorway split down the middle with two significant moments in one's life. On one side lay my high school friends, memories that I will always cherish, and the pinnacle of my adolescent youth I was just not prepared to say good-bye to. The other side whispered promises of an auspicious future, the college experience that is drinking until you pass out, and making new friends in a new environment, all while finding my passion.

It has been one semester since this transition, yet only now do I find myself in the right headspace to give recognition to this step that is a part of everyone's life; its due diligence. I am writing this book for every senior who didn't get a prom. Every senior who didn't get a graduation ceremony. Every senior who was given a "Congrats to the Class of 2020" via Zoom in exchange for the priceless adventures that never were. I hope all of you can relate, at some level, to the following entries.

On another note, if you are steadily approaching the end of high school, take heed to what I am about to say. Savor the mornings when you pull into the school parking lot at 7:00 a.m., wishing you could be anywhere else. Take in the frivolous gossip that is never ceasing. Enjoy all the times you ignorantly believed you and your friends were the only people who mattered. These are the days you will look back on with a grin, realizing how far you've actually come.

I'll leave you with this. When entering one door before shutting another, you risk the likelihood of never gaining closure. Learn from these stories, avoid the same mistakes I made, and if nothing else, know I wrote them on account of everyone who went through what I did this past year.

Journal 1

Spot 1138

It was a warm August day when I painted my senior parking spot. Well, the day my girlfriend painted my senior parking spot. The staff encouraged us to paint something unique to us that symbolized the different attributes we collectively brought to the school. I drove around, tapping on my squeaky brakes every so often to see what others were painting. Some girls were so unoriginal as to just paste their names on the slabs of asphalt. The quirkier ones painted memes of Shrek and SpongeBob, while the rest decided to write corny lines like "Princess parking only" that could've been taken straight from a thirteen-year-old's Instagram bio. Although the guys weren't much better. Most chose not to do one at all, while the ones who did merely spray-painted their name in gold. In this situation, the seniors with girlfriends prevailed, and I was no exception. My girlfriend at the time had an eye for detail but never liked to admit it. That Sunday afternoon, my parking spot transformed from a faded American flag, with holes of asphalt peeking through, to a tapestry resembling my unique past. The center of the parking spot was the state of Texas presented in a coat of shimmering white paint. Inside of Texas was my school's emblem—a golden *R* identical to that of Rice University. Behind this was a matte-black coating, and as simple as it was, it was one of the more original concepts.

Of course, I had driven since sophomore year, but it wasn't until I had a fixed spot that the mornings were something to look forward to. This parking spot was where I would have the first ten minutes of silence to myself at the start of each day. Spot 1138 was also right next to my girlfriend's spot; she would wait on me even when I was running late. It was surrounded by cigarette butts and Juul pods, and it was chipped away ever so slightly when it rained, but there was an invisible beauty that lay beneath its surface. It served as a perfect vantage point for entry into the weight room and was close enough to walk to after practice. It was placed right next to where the snowplow trucks stopped when they would clear the parking lot, creating a massive pile of snow that would prove useful when a snowball fight would break out before the start of school. It bore witness to when my friend Edward, who would go on to win the senior superlative best smile, painted the window of a teacher's car for parking in his spot. This parking spot also sat adjacent to the one-way exit that was used after school, creating an opportunity for me to simply pull straight forward to avoid the collection of cars every day after school. It was an oasis amid a warzone.

It never failed to amuse me to watch how the sophomore students struggled to get their cars started in the bleakness of winter or how aggravating it was to see the wrestling coach pull his lifted Ford F-250 over the yellow line, leaving just enough room for me to squeeze through my door. I fondly remember the times where the latest rumors were spilled on the hood of my car while I got my backpack out of the back seat. It was these simple pleasures, like the walk to the front door with my girlfriend beside me, that now seem glorious when compared to the solitary walks at Wherewithal University under the orange-tented streetlights and slabs of navy-blue concrete that pool in the center when it rained ever so slightly.

My parking spot was where each daily journey as a senior would begin and finish. It was the quintessence of the support, colleagues, and lifelong friends I had literally a car length away from me. These same friends are now scattered across the country, attending universities fifty times the size of our quaint high school tucked away among the cornfields. Other classmates have jobs, some do drugs, some have kids, and some balance all three.

Spot 1138 started the year with a fresh coat of paint. Gradually, rain, snow, and tire marks left behind from burnouts ate away at this coat, and when it was time to graduate, my parking spot was no longer recognizable. Streaks of paint ran down the edges and cracks in the asphalt split Texas down the middle, and the moment the senior class threw our caps in the air, it was no longer mine. That fall, a different design was cast onto the spot. It was time for someone else to paint their legacy and for me to move on with mine.

Fake It till You Make It

My tires squealed to a halt as I pulled into the mostly vacant parking lot located next to the television station. The day had come to return my gear. I turned my head to the back seat of the car to double-check that I had everything with me one last time. Camera? Check. Tripod? Check. Intern ID? It all checked out. Similar to the back seat of my rattletrap silver Volvo, my gear was far from perfect; however, this was why it was all the more painful to give back. There was a mix of innocence and ignorance felt about my rinky-dink equipment. Prior to my internship at my local television station, I had not yet discovered my love for video production. I was given a Sony composite camcorder and was expected to write, produce, film, edit, and air unique content on a biweekly basis. This was very intimidating to someone with no experience, so for the first few weeks, I faked it till I made it; but from then on, I was producing videos with quality unprecedented to those of any intern before me. I turned my head back around, cut the gas, and pulled the keys out of the ignition. As my hands rested on the steering wheel, I sat there for a solid sixty seconds just to take it in one last time. Graduation had come and gone, and it was the next logical step to move forward, but I could not help myself from reminiscing on how far I had progressed since the start of it all.

I opened the door directly behind the driver's side and hoisted the tripod over my shoulder. I then picked up the camera and put the ID lanyard around my neck. That annoying lanyard scratched the back of my neck and irritated every hair follicle that it grazed. I headed for the door, and to my surprise, my ID card did not work. There was no way to get inside any entrance to the building. I panicked because this was my only opportunity to return my equipment.

I was going to college the next morning, and there was no other time for me to stop by. Luckily, the receptionist was just clocking out and let me in through the double-wide door. We both smiled and gave a subtle nod as we passed one another. The heavy door slammed shut behind me and clicked as the deadbolt shifted into place. Moments later, I heard the sound of the receptionist's Jaguar start and tinkle ever so slightly as if it were being deprived of its regular oil change. The parking lot that was mostly empty was now desolate, excluding my vehicle. The lights were turned off, and the cubicles were clear. I was all alone.

When walking past the receptionist's desk, I noticed a brown stain in the shape of a circle on her desk. This was all that remained of her cup of coffee that morning. I then made my way for the basement, which was where a majority of my work was completed. With each descending step down the flight of stairs, the odor of mildew and dust was impossible to ignore. It circulated throughout the air, making it difficult to breathe. It sagged from the ceiling, causing the tiles to cave in, but what more could I ask for in a television station den?

I placed my gear on the lifeless acrylic desk. My sticky notes with video ideas, passwords, and even drawings had all been thrown away. I could not fight the temptation to log on to my computer for the final time to review all the work I had done, which only made things worse. Going through the collection of videos I had amassed by the end of the year was even more excruciating than turning in my camera. The truth was hard to swallow, and in my case, these videos were going to be wiped or lost in storage in a matter of weeks. Their time in the spotlight faded right before my very eyes. A voice crept into my head and said, "You are no longer needed." I could not stand to be at my desk any longer. I didn't even recognize it anymore. The creativity and energy created in that room were erased without me ever knowing.

However, when looking back on the countless hours spent creating new videos and the process of learning how to edit, these skills eventually blossomed into me finding my future. Without this internship, I am not so sure that I would be attending Wherewithal

University or even studying liberal arts. The strange part about this unsatisfying and incomplete goodbye was that it didn't accurately convey my experience there. My boss would greet me every day as I would walk into the building, my superiors would help me with any problem I bumped into, and the videos I made were the staple of my acceptance into the Media Fellows program at Wherewithal. It was all so bizarre and almost seemed more like a nightmare than reality.

I was in complete darkness, only guided by the light peering in through the bottom of the door. When walking back outside, I noticed it was now twilight. I hopped inside my car, and the dash read that it was 8:47 p.m. I knew I had to get home soon because my ex-girlfriend, Jennifer, and I had agreed to say our goodbyes before I left in the morning. I had ripped her heart out three months before in hopes of finding my higher calling at school. She was the only piece of high school that bothered sticking around, but how was I going to rise to the next occasion if I was still holding onto the past? I pulled out of the parking lot and watched through the rearview mirror as the building that once stood prominently slowly vanished into oblivion.

I was close to halfway home when I stopped at a red light and realized that there was no music playing. Wild thoughts had been swarming inside my head for entirely too long. I needed to unwind and free my mind. Plugging in my auxiliary, I was feeling rather introspective and thought of a song I had not heard in over a year. That same voice in my head that had criticized me earlier told me to play "Free Bird" by Lynyrd Skynyrd. I had only heard the song a handful of times before this and knew none of the words. All I knew was that it fit the vibe. The song lasted me the whole way home; I even remember having to cut the song off before it had time to finish playing, resulting in an abrupt, almost dissatisfying ending. As I pulled into the driveway, I could not help but fixate on the lyrics: "If I leave here tomorrow, would you still remember me?" Was this all a colossal coincidence? Was it God trying to reach through to me? I did not have time to think about these scenarios. It was 9:00 p.m., and I saw Jennifer's headlights from across the street. She was right on time, per usual.

She parked parallel to my car as we both debated on whose car to sit in. After a few minutes of friendly chitchat, I submitted to her polite request to sit in the passenger seat of her car. While inside, we both sat there waiting for the other to break the ice that had built up for the past nine weeks. I started off with some nonchalant banter that led to one-word responses, such as "How was your day?"

"Fine."

"Okay, how have you been?" I asked, attempting to revive our once shared connection.

"Good," she responded, which was an emphatic and blatant lie. I could visibly see she yearned for something more. This small talk had not only dulled our new perceptions of each other, but it simply just wasn't what we were accustomed to. This cumbersome conversation had now died off into utter silence.

This was embarrassing. I could not even speak to the same person I called my significant other less than three months ago. There was nothing left to say other than the obvious. The exact reason I called it quits was now barreling toward me and would be inevitable in twelve hours. The tricky part about wanting to rise to those occasions meant cutting off the most important person in my life up to this point. I was divided because one part of me never wanted to leave in the first place, but in order for me to achieve my calling in media, which I found while at my internship, I knew I needed to leave my almost saccharine past behind. I was going to have to trade in the comfort zone I had built up for the past three years for the cold and brutal awakening that was college if I were to come anywhere close to my aspirations. Knowing I wouldn't get a second chance to be with her, I said what we were both thinking.

"I know you still care about me, and I just wanted to let you know I feel the same." I may have caught her off guard because she seemed shocked. Before she could even respond, I continued by saying, "Just because I leave tomorrow doesn't mean we can't be ourselves tonight."

She agreed, and we began to get more personal. Our exchange evolved into what our interests were and what we planned to do without the other around. These were not easy topics to discuss; however, they were necessary for closure. What was originally supposed to be a fifteen-minute goodbye turned into an hour and a half therapy session. The sun had set long ago, and the overcast obstructed any view of the stars. The moon was our only source of light as it shimmered through the gloomy clouds. By the end of our endeavor, we had both relieved one another and assured each other everything was going to be fine. After we had exhausted our heart-to-heart, we both stepped out of her car.

I embraced her and held her closely. Her hair still smelled the same from the lemon-scented shampoo she showered with. Her hoodie was a blend of cotton and cashmere that felt inviting yet so tender. With her head buried in my shoulder, she wept uncontrollably, which caused me to do the same. The tears trickled down the side of my face where they met the corners of my lips. The warm saltwater spoiled the gravity of the situation. By the time we had finished, both of our eyes were a sickly red. As sincere as our goodbye was, it came to an abrupt and unsatisfying end. There was no grand finale or final moment that brought everything to an astounding conclusion. Her presence said more, and we both knew what the other was thinking.

"This is goodbye, I guess," she said in a subtle tone indicating torment.

"I'll see you again," I said, not knowing how to respond. This made it all the more heartbreaking to see her drive away.

Standing still and clutching my car keys in the driveway, I was left with yet another unsatisfying conclusion that night. It was not right for me to put her through that; she deserved better. Here I was embarking on a new adventure; meanwhile, she was expected to stay put in the same town, with the same people, and not say a word. One half of me wanted to call her and tell her to turn around, but deep down, I knew that we would only hold each other back. I stared at my screen for a while before I put it back in my pocket. I entered and closed the front door behind me. I wasn't even five feet from the door before my mom chimed in.

"Where have you been?" she asked with one eyebrow raised slightly. She was staying with me at my aunt and uncle's for the week in preparation of my departure.

I responded under my breath. "Outside."

She could tell I was not myself and wasn't going to pry to find out why. I moped upstairs into my room and lay on my bed. My conscience pleaded that I interact with my mother before the night was over. Ever since the move from Houston, Texas, to Rochester, Indiana, three years ago, my encounters and interactions with my mother were seldom. I will never forget resenting my previous high school so greatly that I was forced to leave without her. Before I could even finish that thought, my phone lit up with a text notification from my mother that read "Come to my room."

My mother was already in her heart-covered pajamas and was covered in the puffy white comforter that lay atop the queen-size mattress. She was propped up with three pillows so that she could watch television but, more importantly, also talk to me. As soon as I entered the room, she turned down the volume to the television and asked a question.

"How are you feeling?" she asked.

I responded with my back to her, as my feet dangled a few inches above the carpeted floor as I sat on the end of the bed. "Honestly, I do not know. Lately, I've felt so astray, as if I'm powerless and cannot do anything about all that is unfolding around me."

She interjected as she sat up. "BJ, no one your age knows what to do right now, and everyone that seems like they do is just faking it. You start a brand-new life tomorrow. Everything you encounter will be unexpected. There is no map on how to live your life. You will try, and sometimes you might fail, but you have to be able to get back up and learn from your mistakes. Do not fret on the future. Instead, be excited about all the possibilities you have at your disposal."

I then turned ninety degrees so the right side of my face was visible to her. The soft sound of the *Wipeout* contestants could be heard when no one was speaking. I had not felt this way since I moved away from Texas, away from my mother, and away from everything I had previously known, in search of a more promising life in Indiana. This was a familiar feeling; it ate away at my inner being for the first semester when I was beginning my fresh start in Indiana. Everything I had built during the last three years was now coming to an abrupt end. I expressed my concerns as I twiddled my thumbs and looked down at my feet.

"I am not worried about the trials and tribulations of tomorrow. I am worried about what I am leaving behind," I said.

Before the move, my résumé was blank, and now, I had accolades: captain of the football team, all-state wide receiver, Key Club president, National Honors Society, and top ten GPA in my class were just some of the titles I held proud. But perhaps the friendships, ties, and roles I played in the community were greater than all those combined. Rochester accepted me as nothing and turned me into someone with a voice that can spark positive change throughout a community. I continued to share my thoughts.

"I know graduating high school is a normal and necessary stepping stone in the grand scheme of things, but it does not mean I have to pretend to enjoy it either. People keep telling me these next few months are the best that will ever happen to me, and I cannot help to think that is blasphemy. I created a legacy here in three short years by starting with nothing besides my name. I found friends. I found love. Hell, I even found a way to solidify my reputation, and now I am supposed to throw that all away? I know leaving was always a part of the plan, but why do I feel so desultory?"

She wasted no time in comforting me with more words of wisdom. I smelled the cherry wine she had with dinner, on her breath as she continued.

"Honey, I know it is hard to compare what you had, along with what you lost. It can feel as if you are straying from the path you shaped yourself, but what you do not realize is that you are still paving the way, except this time, your path will have an undecided destination. When you first moved to Indiana, while you did not have much, you knew who you wanted to be. This time around, you may not know who you want to be, and that is okay." I was now facing her. She knew she had won me over, which was apparent by her subtle smirk. I stayed and watched television with her until midnight but cut it off after that because I knew I had to be up early.

I was now back in my bathroom brushing my teeth and staring at my reflection. I was a pale, nervous wreck. The two things keeping me awake were my sharp mint-flavored Colgate toothpaste and the frigid marble countertop my hands were resting upon. I knew what lay ahead were weeks searching for friends and finding my identity on campus. While my mother's advice helped, it was not going to quench my thirst for acceptance and purpose. I needed something physical and concrete today—a task, a new friend, or something to latch on and immerse myself in—but deep down, I knew that was problematic. My mother always mentioned there was a downside to being as driven as I am. Fear of the unknown plagued my mind that night. I tossed and turned while allowing every emotion to race through my body. Fear, anxiety, and depression formed the three-headed monster that doubted my every move. I was my own worst enemy.

My alarm echoed throughout my room and cued the start to the day that would change my life forever. I was awake before anyone else. I stepped into the shower and put on the clothes I had laid out the night before. A quick breakfast consisting of Fruity Pebbles was all I had an appetite for. I didn't even have time to put down the bowl of the sugary cereal I had poured, so there were a few stragglers left when I placed it in the sink. My mother was not far behind, although all she desired was a cup of coffee. As for my grandmother, she and my mother planned to ride down together, which left me in my car driving down solo. It was not long before my grandmother arrived with a carload of my things to take with me to college.

"You got everything?" my grandmother questioned as she fidgeted with the window. My mother assured her we did. She then climbed into my grandmother's white Ford Edge and backed out of our driveway as I followed closely behind. The forecast was partly cloudy with a chance of thunderstorms. Even the weather was uncertain of its next move. We left at 9:06 a.m., and my grandmother squabbled about how we were going to be late despite being only two and a half hours away. My neighbors waved casually, not knowing that this would be the last time they would see me for the foreseeable future. I drove down Main Street and gazed at the landmarks that made the town what it was. I soberly cruised by the city limit sign. It felt as if I deserted the town that gave me a second chance. Every mile I pulled away pulled a little more on my heartstrings. The trek started very tediously. It felt as if I were on the road for hours before even getting past Peru, Indiana. The construction in Kokomo only magnified the urge to turn around. I admired the view of endless emerald-green cornstalks as their golden tassels drifted in the breeze. My grandmother took the wrong exit in Indianapolis, causing me to crash back down to reality. This forced me to circumnavigate my way through Indianapolis traffic by myself and even at one point stumbled upon a road sign that read "Wrong way, turn around." Oh, how easy that would be. However, for better or for worse, I finally saw the Wherewithal University highway sign. I exited right and entered Sheetzville, Indiana. It was not time for me to check in yet, so my mother suggested we go eat at Buffalo Wild Wings. I pulled into the first parking space I could find and got a table inside. It was time for the last supper.

"So a lemonade, iced tea, and water then," the waitress said with a pen and pad in hand.

"Yes," I said under my mask.

"Okay, I'll have that right out for you," she said as she walked toward the kitchen. I browsed the menu as the waitress slid past the swinging doors. The enticing smell of spices carried throughout the dining area, but I still had no appetite. My mother and grandmother sat on one end, while I sat on the other. My mother started another conversation.

"Are you ready?" she asked.

"As ready as I'll ever be." I insisted. I could not believe I was going to be on campus within the hour. I peered at my grandmother and mother as they chatted away about my younger cousin's softball game they were going to attend after they dropped me off. *Drop me off,* I thought. We were talking about me going to college, and they were treating it as if I needed a ride to the airport. I knew it was not their fault they could only stay an hour, but the stigma surrounding the situation was inexcusable in my opinion. I felt like a baby bird getting thrown from the nest, having to fend for myself. I also knew college was about finding my own way, and eventually, I would; but for now, why was this process so abrasive? I was furious and eventually wore myself out balancing all the hypotheticals. All this time spent thinking was time wasted I could have been sharing with those whom I cared about. My internal clock continued ticking, counting every second left until we were separated. Our meals were brought out to us with roughly forty minutes to spare. My lemonade glass had begun to condensate, and my honey-barbecue wings were brought out cold. None of that mattered. What mattered was enjoying the last few minutes I had with my family, even if every emotion within me said otherwise. Our minuscule meal was short but sweet. The one thing I coveted more of, was the one thing I could not have, time. We had now finished the meal and had ten minutes to be at Blackhawk Stadium. We left a tip for the server and were on our way. I jumped inside my car and knew from this moment on, nothing would be the same.

I made it on time and was instantly greeted by a series of questions pertaining to COVID-19.

"Have you experienced shortness of breath within the last forty-eight hours?"

"No."

"How about congestion or a runny nose?"

"No."

"Any nausea or vomiting?"

"No," I said, for what felt like the tenth time in a row.

These questions persisted for the next several minutes. Meanwhile, from my peripheral vision, I caught a glimpse of my grandma being subjugated to the same interrogation.

Out of all the years to go to college, this had to be the one. I was born less than a month after 9/11, and now I was attending my first year of college during a global pandemic. My timing for life-changing events was impeccable. After the infrared thermometer gun scanned my forehead, I was cleared to pass. It took me all forty-five seconds to get to the Hugh Jassol lot. Right before I pulled in, a woman requested that I roll down my window.

"You have one hour. Do you understand?"

"Yes," I said, as my eyes rolled to the back of my skull. My grandma and I found a couple of parking spots on the very end with a car in between the two of them. I instantly opened her trunk and started unloading the black-and-yellow totes from her car. As I attempted to go find where the luggage carts might be, my grandmother complained that it was hot outside and that she needed to sit down someplace cool. The humidity had climbed at an alarming rate; it was now a sweltering ninety-three degrees according to my weather app. I swiftly ushered her to the Cam Hulltoe Hall lobby. As I grasped her clammy hands, she plopped into a padded seat. She ended up being fine; she just needed to rest for a few minutes and cool down. My mother looked over her as I went to go claim my own luggage cart.

Eventually, I found the tent where the carts were and, seconds later, was wheeling a wobbling cart down the crooked red brick sidewalk. Per usual, three wheels cooperated fine, while the back-left wheel spiraled uncontrollably. I had fit about half of my totes and personal items in the cart, and I thought that I only needed one more trip down, and I would be done in ten minutes. What was taking people so long? I quickly came to the conclusion that the cart was only useful for the trip from the car to the front entrance of Cam Hulltoe Hall. I came to a halt at the concrete steps that prevented me from moving my cart into the lobby, and even then, I wouldn't have made it much farther due to the elevator coincidentally being out of service. I pushed the impractical cart aside as I grabbed my twenty-seven-inch Roku television and the largest tote I could carry. As I entered the lobby, my grandmother followed directly behind me. One foot after another, I scaled the glossy staircase. I passed signs that read "Down only" and thought to myself, *Bite me.* I was panting heavily between the weight of my tote and television by the time I reached the fourth floor. The white cloth mask that covered my face did not help either, as it had my face turning a bright blue. The bottoms of my sneakers rubbed smoothly across the revolting red-and-green-striped carpet as I found my way to dorm 407.

The butterflies that had been building up all day were ready to be released. I set my items down and grabbed the golden key from the manila folder that was given to me at check-in. My right hand shook violently, and I inserted it into the keyhole. With a simple clockwise turn, I put my foot in the door that was going to propel me into the next four years.

"You have got to be joking" were the first words that came out of my mouth.

"It is not that bad," my grandmother said reassuringly. My mother then arrived on the scene and bore witness to the aftermath that accompanied my initial reaction.

The ceiling caved in, leaving a foot of headspace above the bed. An electrical rod stuck out of the wall above the doorframe. The remains of what appeared to be a functional fire alarm were reduced to a circular metal frame bolted into the wall with wires emerging out of it. This alone was enough to request a room change even before taking into account the amount of livable space I had available to me. My dorm was sixty-four square feet. The space remaining after accounting for the furniture was a fourteen-by-two runway that stretched from the closet to the window. I noticed another door that stood at the foot of the bed frame. Could this be a double divided by a door? Was it another single that would not be occupied this semester? Perhaps I was too harsh in judging my accommodations. Of course, this positive train of thought would backfire moments later when I heard the sound of someone moving into the neighboring room.

The walls were paper-thin. I could hear every word of every conversation; privacy was completely absent. It was at this point when my mother became more enraged than I already was.

"You should be paying half price for this prison cell," she cried hysterically. She left the dungeon in a blaze of fury to search for an advisor, leaving my grandmother and me behind to sulk in her fiery wake. My grandmother sat down in the desk chair and was too exhausted to move until it was time to leave. How did I know that despite bringing two people to help me move in that it was going to ultimately be me who carried all my belongings up the four flights of stairs? Fifteen miserable trips later, I had finally moved everything inside my miniature dorm. My family and I started to unpack my clothes and figured out how to utilize as much space as possible. We threw my dresser and shelf under the bed and started rearranging my dorm when there was an unanticipated knock at my door. I opened the door to see two resident advisors who questioned me as soon as we made eye contact.

"Hey, we just wanted to make sure you are following the guidelines and staying on the time schedule. What was your check-in time?"

"One thirty," I said with an infuriating undertone. One of the advisors promptly responded.

"Oh, that is too bad. Unfortunately, since it is now two forty-five and you are fifteen minutes over the hour timeslot, we are going to have to ask your family to leave the premises." I didn't even give them the pleasure of showing how much that single request got under my skin. I didn't even respond. I nodded as my grandmother pushed her chair in and my mother laid down one of my collared shirts. Several totes, boxes, and containers were piled on top of one another, unopened, as my dorm lay barren.

"Do you want to walk us out?" my mother questioned.

"Yeah, I will walk you out," I said. I held the door open as we proceeded to walk to the car. On our way out, we passed two peppy sophomore girls greeting first-year students and listening to Bruno Mars's "Locked Out of Heaven."

"Well, it looks like we are here," my mother teased. While she did put a smile on my face under my mask, I could not joke back. My grandmother hugged me and then spoke as she stepped away.

"I love you and will miss you," she said, struggling not to show too much emotion. She then opened up her door and sat inside the car as my mother and I shared our last exchange.

"You will do great things here, BJ. I am so proud of you!" she exclaimed. I frantically pondered what to say back. The colloquial "I love you" was not enough. It could not come close to capturing what I was feeling. No, instead, the final words I said to my mother when we were face-to-face was something that could not be answered.

"What do I do?"

"Go explore. The world is yours," she professed. Tears once again flooded my eyes. I was too choked up to say anything else. She pulled me in, and we hugged each other for the last time. She rolled her window down and waved as my grandmother backed out and pulled onto East Concord Street. I watched as they turned left at the intersection leading toward New Residence Hall 1. Hats off to Wherewithal—they were undefeated in the naming department. Still clutching onto my room key, I went to the only place I saw fit—back to my dorm.

Once there, I closed the door behind me. The room was completely silent. There was no commotion of other first years moving in and no noises of the guy next door. It was just me surrounded by blank walls and unopened boxes. Should I start putting away clothes? Should I start sorting the snacks I packed? Do I do anything at all? The thought of calling Mom or Grandma was enticing, but I knew I had to figure this problem and the rest of them out on my own. I walked over to an unopened box on the ground and started sorting the scattered mess that was my dorm.

Later that day, I met several students on the front lawn of Cam Hulltoe Hall. These people were a part of my mentor group, which was instructed by a sophomore student. They were from places all over the country. I listened as they explained.

"California."

"Chicago."

"Sheetzville."

It didn't matter where they were from. They all seemed to have it together, and there I was, lost and tempest-tossed. Was I being too hard on myself? Why did everyone seem so confident with their whereabouts? Perhaps they were just faking it, or maybe I just needed to do the same.

Presented by the Illustrious Class of 2020

Thursday, March 12, 2020, was the last time we would see each other
without our caps
There was no warning, no notice, no indication of this collapse
What's one extra week tacked on to spring break?
Give it three weeks, and this headache will pass, make no mistake
Television and radio ads saying, "Congratulations to the Class of
2020" stand in place for what could've been
Dreams of senior prom and girls wearing animal skin
There is no replacing the years spent anticipating, waiting for that
single song
The one that would confirm your suspicions of that special someone
all along
It's only a couple of months we missed out on, who are we kidding
These last few months were the only thing shielding us from expec-
tations that are so unforgiving
I remember afternoons in the parking lot when the seventh-period
bell rang
Subtle frustrations and pent-up anxiety came out through the tail-
pipes of Mustangs
We were born from the ashes of those fateful towers
Then graduated during a pandemic that stripped us of what was
rightfully ours
Perhaps we were cursed from the very beginning
We grew up a part of the generation obsessed with self-image, con-
formity, and boomerangs captioned #twinning

It will be hard to top receiving my diploma via drive-thru
Or the weeks spent in AP Gov, studying judicial review
The thing that scares me the most is the fact there is no redo
The distant sporadic nights when we'd all squeeze into one car will have to make do
It is painful to think our legacy will be boiled down to the class of COVID
Society's branding as such has been duly noted; but what if it didn't have to be?
And we instead remembered what it was like before the debris
When our biggest fears were being tardy and bad hair days
Or the times we all fought the uphill battle that was putting off an essay
Somewhere lay the vague memories we all share
Like staring out the classroom window, longing for a breath of fresh air
I know I'm not the only one struggling to say goodbye
To the expired sourdough the cafeteria used to supply
Don't even think about putting a price on those Friday-night lights
Watching the team run out of the tunnel was an unbelievable sight
The athletic director was notorious for taking the joy out of any sporting event
So we'd fire back and always mention how he still lived in his mother's basement
These are the moments I look back and reminisce
Because I know in a few short years, credit card debt, a marriage on the cusp of divorce, and daydreams of retirement will only persist
Wouldn't it be great if we could all go back?
No, I don't mean the reunions that people try too hard at or the red punch and faint smells of bleached floors mixed in with lilac
I mean, go back to sign each other's yearbook and embrace our friends before we bid adieu
Minus the acne, heavy textbooks, and sophomoric rumors that were untrue
On the horizon rests something that will forever be out of reach

Must closure have to be beseeched?
I know it is only a matter of time before my classmates and I leave the
    cliché social cliques and aspirations of dating the prom queen
    behind
But for now, is it all right if we relish the last of our moribund
    juvenescence?

Last Day

The day that would live in infamy had arrived. Every senior, every student, pulled into the parking lot clueless of the abrupt demise that would purloin their precious adolescence. We all carried our books into class and rolled our eyes at the monotone lectures we had grown accustomed to over the last four years, unaware that they'd be our last. We laughed and took for granted the childish anecdotes we all shared at the lunch table etched in graffiti. Every single one of us were just anticipating the weekend.

I pulled away from the school, as I did every day, to go to my internship, and after scanning my keycard, I walked into the basement to find health workers in white hazmat suits spraying down every doorknob and keyboard. COVID-19 was on everyone's radar, but at this point in time, it wasn't much more than a talking point on the nightly news. I barely managed to squeeze past one of them before finding my black office chair on wheels. I only had the chance to login to the intern-specific desktop before I heard my boss knock twice on the wooden door with the knuckle of his index finger. His distorted voice was difficult to hear given all the background noise the sanitation crew was creating, but we both took turns shouting over each other.

"Hey, BJ, we're going to have you leave early today," he said, leaning his head through the open door.

"All right, I'm going to take a shot in the dark and guess it's because the entire place is being disinfected?" I asked, logging back out of my computer.

"Hit the nail on the head, champ," he said, smiling.

"Okay, and then what? Meet you back here tomorrow same time?" I asked, grabbing my backpack and standing up.

"Actually, no, I'm not sure when we'll be back here in person," he said. "It's probably best if you stay at school these next few days before spring break, and we can reassess our timeline then."

"All right. That puts me behind in scheduling, but I guess I can work around it," I said, naive as can be.

"Don't worry about that. We'll see you back here after spring break, okay?" he said, ushering me outside. That would be the last time I'd see him until graduation, but his five-o'clock shadow, fatherly demeanor, and casual Friday attire, not dependent on what day of the week it was, would follow me for months. I fastened my seat belt and picked out a song for the three-minute drive back to the school. The afternoons spent listening to *Flower Boy* and watching the samaras glide past my windows as I followed the back roads to school never grew old. Although this afternoon didn't follow in their succession.

I noticed a crowd of students pouring out of the building as I passed the track and football stadium. Buses were lined up and running as freshmen boarded them. School wasn't supposed to finish for another thirty minutes, and track practice wasn't supposed to start for another forty-five. My initial thought was one my parents never would have thought of in their day. *What would it be this time, a bomb threat or potential shooter?* As sad as it is, this is a reality our generation is far too familiar with. But seeing as how calm everyone was, I knew this couldn't have been the case.

I parked my car and cut the gas to see even more students piling on top of one another. In all my time at Rochester, this had been the first early release I had ever seen, and under normal circumstances, they would have come before a holiday, not on the Thursday a week before spring break. Then I remembered what had driven me out of the television station. *Could COVID-19 already be upon us?* I grabbed my duffel bag that had a change of clothes and a pair of track spikes in them and headed for the door. I was the only one going inside and may have brushed against half of the student body before making it past the doors. I was met with disgruntled shoulder checks and smart remarks every step of the way until I heard the principal's commands echo on the intercom.

"Clear everything out of your lockers. Treat this as if it was the last day before summer. And get outside." By the time he had finished his dramatic monologue, I had already made it to the track locker room located inside the gymnasium, and as far as I knew, practice was still on. The doors were locked, but I hadn't received any emails that called off practice. This entire ordeal was becoming more and more unclear. When I turned around, Ryan Helt, the head track coach, was standing behind me. We stood and listened as the principal came back for an encore. In addition to regurgitating the same information he had repeated numerous times, he clarified by mentioning that after-school practices were still a go, and we needed to do our best not to feel perturbed. Hard to believe when we evacuated the school as if an EF5 tornado was on a collision course with the cafeteria. Helt and I just stood there facing one another as he appeared to be just as puzzled as me. He then shrugged and was speechless as to what to say. We were chess pieces standing there across from each other on the polished basketball court inside an empty gymnasium. It was almost as if every move and every scenario all led back to that position in time. That was when I knew my reign in Rochester was at its end. There was no avoiding the realistic wave of melancholy and mediocrity headed my way. It was going to shake all my classmates to their cores regardless. It was time to grow up. Whether we liked it or not, we were being shoved from the nest, and with that came the harsh revelation of learning that nothing in life is promised.

There was no fairytale Disney ending waiting for my classmates and me. Nowhere was it stated that once we finished high school, we'd all break out into song and perform an intricate dance routine while we threw our caps in the air. There was no grand finale where the guy got the girl and kissed her as the screen faded to black. Alternatively, I was greeted with an end to my senior track season before I even had a chance to break the school record in the four hundred meter. I had always yearned for an opportunity to be remembered for years to come. Unfortunately, that would come at a steep price. What I didn't realize is that there is one commonality with every person who has ever been remembered. Sacrifice. From TikTokers selling away their ideologies for a little bit of clout to child actors giving their innocence away for fame, every single individual commonly known by the public has sacrificed in one way or another. If my name was going to be on that record board above the concession stand, I was going to have to sacrifice the unborn memories with friends that could only take place during spring after school, and I was okay with that. And while I never got a chance to be remembered for that reason, my entire class will be remembered. Our muzzled faces paired with our mortarboards will live in textbooks for decades to come, but I didn't think anyone of us would truly be able to grasp what we all sacrificed. Sure, you could put a price on the short sparkling dresses the volleyball team wore or the ninety-nine cent Hawaiian Punch everyone refuses to touch but had there ever been an authentic substitute to these tacky moments?

After practice, I hunkered down at my grandma's until spring break arrived. Dead-end emails and humdrum announcements flooded my inbox with nothing to show. Administration had not yet declared the status of the school, and soon wouldn't even have the authority to do so, but somehow, I knew there was only one way for this to end. Knowing I'd either be held hostage or be putting my grandmother at risk by leaving the house every day, I decided to go to Houston. It might not have been the brightest option, but it was the better of the two.

There, I retreated to a family friend's property to finish schooling. The property was on the outskirts of College Station, and when I wasn't on a Zoom call, I was pitching scrap metal with the only friend in Texas who never turned his back on me, Justin. He wept when I left but was always there to pick me up from the airport when I'd visit. He and I were basically sons to my mother's friend who owned the property. We would always crash at her property when the city life grew dull so long as we lent a helping hand.

It was on the official last day of school when I had to give a ten-minute speech covering a subject I can't even remember. My English instructor, Mrs. Hoover, congratulated us on our astounding achievement while her facial expressions lagged from one frame to the next and her audio cut in and out. I never understood why we depended on Zoom so heavily when Google Meet was the far superior program, but that was beside the point. My teacher was hardly recognizable, and her robotic pitch sounded nothing like her bubbly voice. After everyone gave their speeches, we all waved and said our goodbyes, unsure if we'd even see each other again. I was the last one to close the window. I had never been good at goodbyes, and staring at my screen that read "Waiting for host to start the meeting" while sitting down in the kitchen was enough to make me beg for just one more day in the hormone-ran jungle that was high school.

Later that day, as the sun began to set, I turned over a piece of sheet metal, disrupting a sleeping copperhead, but it never leapt at me or hissed. It just sat there wallowing in fear while it tried to burrow itself once more. I planned on leaving it alone, but the ranch hand who was also helping out Justin and me insisted I kill the innocent creature. In no more than a few seconds, I separated its head from its body with the end of a shovel. It was swift, but it wasn't fair. The snake continued to twitch as its reflexes slowly burned out. I sometimes wonder if any of us could be that snake. We were all kids once, riding on the backs of shopping carts with absolutely no direction. We then slowly sprouted and started to test the waters with our new-found knowledge. Then somewhere along the line, we grew out of this. We found our identities while attending class seven times a day and being served cauliflower at 11:00 a.m. But even that wouldn't be the end. We'd eventually trade our hometown hospitality for a college education. We'd then move to a big city in hopes of climbing the corporate ladder. Years would pass as bonuses, promotions, and the desire to one-up Kim from across the street claimed any and all physical evidence of our remaining pixie dust. The time had come. The final bell dismissing school had rung.

We have already been robbed of our youth. The only ending even more unsatisfying than the one we've been dealt would be to trade the values and lessons we've learned along the way in exchange for the same incentives that have been draining the working class of anything remotely close to happiness. Don't play into anyone's hand but your own. There is magic in the talent shows where the quirky kid plays the Minecraft theme on the piano. There is humor in jokes made by your AP American Studies teacher who says, "Now, kids, this isn't a political statement" or when your English teacher blares the scene from *The Big Bang Theory* that shows Sheldon shouting, "Do not stop refreshing your screens!" when she made an update on the agenda. Okay, so maybe that is just me, but there is innocence in obtaining your driver's license and something endearing about choosing to be late to first period in favor of a trip to Dunkin' Donuts.

The Class of 2020 will go down in history. Not for being the class that made it through a pandemic. Not for being the Zoom guinea pigs. Not even for being the class to attend their first year of college online. We will be remembered as the class who never lost their spark. We will be the class to redefine what it means to grow up. Lastly, you can be sure we will be remembered for our individuality. May the Class of 2020 never forget how to fly.

Orientation

A few days had gone by since the first meeting of my first-year mentor group. Outside of the awkward mandatory social luncheons, we ate anywhere but inside; there wasn't a heck of a lot to do. Classes didn't start until the thirty-first, the following Monday, and at the time, it was only Thursday. Before the pandemic, water balloon fights, color runs, fireworks, movie nights, concerts, and yes, even bouncy houses were all activities available to the incoming students. With those events now completely out of the question, Wherewithal was in desperate need of finding something to keep us occupied while also making us feel at home. After the university's leading panelists and board of directors spent months mapping out freshmen orientation, they had finally unveiled the simple solution that would stand in place of the usual festivities. Zoom. Ah, yes, so simple. It was right in front of our noses. Why waste time coming up with socially distant outdoor activities when you could isolate every student in their dorms who all breathed through the same ventilation system?

Every single event, gathering, meeting, party, and occasional exercise session would take place on our computers. Although I wasn't able to try most exercises, taking into consideration my wingspan stretched from wall to wall. Events like the virtual meet and greets held by the RAs were optional, but the school-wide meetings that reviewed Title IX and the COVID-19 Policy Handbook were mandatory. These meetings were held online; however, each mentor group had a designated classroom around campus that would serve as a venue for these webinars. Most of these classrooms would remain vacant for the next year but were completely full for orientation, which only made the decision not to have in-person classes for an entire year seem all the more ass-backward. My guess was that the school wanted to make sure we were all actually there instead of allowing us to hide behind the black screens that appeared when our cameras weren't on while we did only-God-knows-what.

Well, whether we liked it or not, the time had come. It was time to meet with our first-year mentor group and attend one of these webinars. Of course, the first one dealt with the one thing on every college kid's mind—sex. More importantly, how to approach it "responsibly." The topic was Title IX, and after watching eight or so scripted videos that were acted out poorly, it was time to talk about what not to do. I would've given anything to have been in one of those bouncy houses. The university encouraged its students to pull out their phones and submit responses to the questions displayed on the screen. A Kahoot! version of consent, if you will.

The first question appeared on the screen and read something along the lines of "What is the proper way to ensure both parties are comfortable with moving forward?"

The responses rang in lightning-fast, and most were totally acceptable. "Are you okay with this?" "Should we take this to my room?" "Do you want to keep going?" But of course, when the moderator started reading the responses out loud, some of the freshmen boys got the bright idea to submit some responses that were NSFW. "You ready for this pipe?" "Girl, you're thicker than a bowl of oatmeal" and "Wanna swallow my seeds?" As revolting as it was, every person was cracking up under their masks. Even the mentors could not hide their amusement.

I expected the moderator to urge them to stop, but shockingly, she seemed to only promote these answers. She agreed that this was appropriate and effective language to emphasize responsible sexual activity; only this time, they became even more vulgar and plentiful. She was throwing gasoline on an already out-of-control wildfire. The next question was in. "What is an effective way of showing someone you're comfortable with sex?"

"What are you doing, put it in already. Harder, harder, and fuck me, Daddy." This could not be happening. I felt like I was in an episode of *South Park*, but that's what happens when you give an entire freshmen class the keys to a meeting about sex. I'm seriously not even sure if the moderator ever realized she was being pranked.

Several painfully inappropriate and hilariously creative comments later, we moved on to the discussion of sexual orientation. While its main focus was to welcome everyone a part of the LGBTQ+ community, the moderator also gave "helpful" tips as to what sex on campus should look like. She started off light by first mentioning how there were rainbow-colored condoms at the wellness center but then went as far as to share with us how to have sex during COVID-19. One-night stands were at the forefront of her agenda and were encouraged passionately. She clarified by stating that one-time relationships should be normalized. This included positions that strayed away from the face-to-face element and were then followed with examples, such as doggy style. Imagine being more concerned about two weeks of quarantine than a lifelong STD. She then noted that we should use masks for the entire duration of intercourse and avoid eye contact or kissing at all costs because why go to first base when you can head straight for home?

It was now dark outside, and after being deterred from any and all moral obligations, I was ready to go back to my closet. I fell asleep that night picturing how my grandmother would have received it and was thankful for all the hindsight a small town like Rochester provided me with, even if it was now only visible from the back of my eyelids.

Journal 2

Close to Home

Sheetzville, Indiana, is a quaint town roughly thirty-eight miles south-west of Indianapolis. Home to Wherewithal University, with young and vibrant college kids roaming free on Saturday nights around the courthouse square, it was not uncommon to see them stumble upon the nostalgic dining experience that was Close to Home. From what started out as a small-sized tearoom, this now fully-fledged restaurant had been bringing authentic home-cooked meals to students who were homesick or just looking for a good meal for over thirty years.

The letters that bore the name were posted above the wooden doorframe on a classic red brick-and-mortar building with a green exterior. The windows had white writing on both sides of the front door showcasing the restaurant's quality by stating "where friends and food meet," "unique ingredients," and "comfort food at its best." Two shaded tables under black umbrellas lay beneath the lighting fixtures grappling to the side of the building for whenever the weather was particularly sublime. Once inside, the diner was divided into three sections that were dependent on the time and occasion. The first section was the one spotted after entering the eatery and passing the old-school vending machine. It was the most casual of the three spaces and the oldest room in the diner. It was mainly used during the midday hours of 11:00 a.m. to 1:00 p.m. and was the relaxed atmosphere a lunch date between two people who claimed to be just friends would employ. The wooden chairs creaked when more pressure was applied to one side of the seat than the other, the decor was barren, and the space itself was very cramped but in a cutesy hometown type of way. Conversations floated around the room and bounced off the light-green concrete flooring. A staircase composed of three carpeted steps was what led into the formal dining room.

The eccentric black-and-gray-squared carpet stretched from one end to the other, passing two brick pillars that divided the room in half. The tables were equipped with white tablecloth and a glass covering on top. Paintings of twentieth-century France cafés set the mood, while sounds of freshly popped corks unveiled the aroma of aged wine.

Most waitresses were in their twenties, had recently graduated, and were doing this until they could find their real calling while also making some money in the meantime. Of course, the enormous cast-iron clock on the wall was a subtle reminder that time doesn't stop for anyone. The silver cutlery that was rolled inside a linen napkin and placed on each table was reminiscent of the newly detached freshman that went there and sought to be coddled once more. The menu was designed to cater to these needs and did so in providing nutritious meals that fueled the mind, body, and soul. Close to Home realized that college kids often settled for instant ramen and fast food or even get tired with the food in the Montgomery Dining Hall, which was exactly why these items were void in place of steak, soups, salads, tenderloin, and desserts galore. With one simple bite of the staple dessert that was strawberry pizza, a student who had been deprived of the simple pleasures in life was instantly transported back home without the need for travel. This tranquil restaurant was an oasis on the outskirts of a bustling college campus, but it was possible for that same student looking for a hearty meal to hear murmurs of the roaring nightlife next door.

The third and final element of this homey diner was the Shaken not Stirred bar that was only lit by neon signs and pendant lights. The bar was covered in Chicago Cubs memorabilia, had several flat-screen televisions, and offered plenty of alcohol to students above the age of twenty-one, most of whom would likely have a hangover the following morning. An average night in the bar consisted of shouting at whatever ballgame was on by drunken townsfolk and students alike with assorted nuts scattered across the bar. Similarities in taste of music, along with the bartender's witty anecdotes, accompanied the fun-loving environment, uniting people of all different backgrounds. Once the night had settled down and the buzz had worn off, realizing

Monday morning was creeping up could be just as difficult as the workweek itself, but there was comfort in knowing that home was right around the corner.

Prom Queen

I know you never got the chance to cap off your run as the four year reigning sex symbol, everyone with a working libido wanted to sleep with, in the shimmering fashion you had once hoped for. I suppose you'll have to find solace in knowing that the vacant gymnasiums, empty ballrooms, and deserted venues never bore witness to your skin-tight slip dress. Pretty ironic to think the day you lived out countless times in your head would be the single one you weren't actually allowed to be a part of. I remember when I first laid eyes on you. Those were the times when you were content with playing cat and mouse and when I took advantage of the times your boyfriend wasn't around. So much has changed since the days I'd do your work for a chance at a Facetime call past nine or a side-hug during passing period. But that's the role of the guy friend, and nobody else fit the description quite as well. I couldn't help but be drawn to those piercing blue eyes and that platinum blonde hair. You knew exactly what you were doing when you wore those mini skirts, didn't you? It's a shame I couldn't wait forever, but then again who knows if we would've lasted anyway. You needed a trophy. Someone chiseled with muscle. Perhaps captain of the basketball team, or maybe the president of his own fan club. Someone with a firm handshake. Someone you bring home to Dad. With all of this being said, I actually look back on those days fondly. Who even knows when we'll cross paths again, but at the very least, can you promise me this

Promise me you won't be the one to peak in high school. Promise me now that we're not confined by the hierarchy of high school, we'll actually stay in touch. Promise me you won't be the one to get pregnant at age twenty-three, consequently giving up on all your hopes and dreams. Promise me you'll get out of this town and never look back because, I assure you, there's more to life than having your name in the paper and face on a billboard. Then again, maybe that's all you're after. My downfall has always been envisioning a better life for the very people who want nothing to do with it, and if we're being honest, what do you have to lose?

No one can take away your little kingdom surrounded by corn-fields. Every housewife will want to be in your inner circle, and every husband will fantasize about the day he gets to have an affair. Well, regardless of what happens, I think my inner fifteen-year-old self will always be a victim of that inescapable seductive spell you managed to cast on me sophomore year. So just remember, I'll always be there. Whether you need someone to come pick you up from your toxic on-again/off-again ex-boyfriend's apartment, or you just need some-one to hold your hair back as you throw up the Jell-O shots someone force-fed you, I'll be there.

When Rural and Unrefined Meet Prep and Congeniality

Earnestmore County, Indiana, was home to the city of Sheetzville and runoff towns of Woodpine and Greendale. The two-lane highway that trickled into Sheetzville had billboards every half-mile with ads for real estate agencies and payday loans. The rolling plains that cascaded from one crop field to the next were home to a few thousand people, most of whom lived paycheck to paycheck. The faces seen around town all blended together; however, the Sheetzville and College Inns always seemed to have one more vacant room, if interested. Lifted trucks with doors not matching the rest of the exterior could be found in about every parking lot. Commerce was scarce, with not much beyond the typical grocery store, fast-food chain, gas station, hospital, post office, or school. Blue-collar jobs claimed a majority of the workforce, seeing as how job listings were often for warehouse associates, delivery drivers, and assembly lines. Residents of Sheetzville typically did not hold a college degree, let alone a master's. Yet despite the meager margin of white-collar job listings and interest in higher learning, a thriving university lay at the heart of the city and was quite the anomaly when compared to the rest of Sheetzville.

As for Wherewithal University, the 655-acre campus was filled with luscious oak and maple trees planted in Bermuda grass lawns, surrounding buildings dedicated to promoting education and an overall understanding of the world outside of Sheetzville. The preeminent buildings pertained to certain fields of study, such as Contemporary Media, Diversity and Inclusion, and the Performing

Arts, while straying far from any establishment or experience available to the public. Now, while these places could pertain to students and their degree track, there were several purely recreational places in or around campus as well. The Cinema was a quaint two-theater complex that showed the newest Hollywood blockbusters. Wherewithal Nature Park was a series of trails all exploring the extension of wilderness the city could not possibly offer. Lastly, the nightlife that was just outside of the university gates differed from what Sheetzville as a city presented. Commercial string lights draped from building to building, highlighting restaurants, such as Big Mouth Burgers, Eazy Freeze Ice Cream Parlor, Close to Home, and Henry's Bar, all around the courtyard square. Obviously, a night-and-day difference compared to the blasé Earnestmore Plaza on the foremost street in the middle of town visible from Kokomo Road, but the gap between Wherewithal and Sheetzville stretched much farther than the dissimilarities in attractions and lifestyle.

Wherewithal was a private university that offered a liberal arts education with students stemming from thirty-four states and nineteen other countries. Diversity was widely noticeable on campus, with many cultures and ethnicities present, including well-represented populations of African Americans, Hispanics, Latinx, and Asian Americans. The GPA requirement to be admitted into Wherewithal was 3.78, along with an SAT score of around 1260 or higher. Clearly, there was a higher standard of education expected from its students than the less-demanding portrayal Sheetzville natives were accustomed to. In addition to this, less than half of all students attending Wherewithal were born in Indiana; meaning, to the larger half of students, Sheetzville, as well as Indiana, was entirely new to them. From the socioeconomic standpoint of students at Wherewithal, the average household income for students was $144,440, with 59 percent of households belonging to the top 20 percent. Less than 1 percent of students came from what the Office of the Assistant Secretary for Planning and Evaluation would classify as a poor family, a household that collected $26,200 annually for a family of four.

It did not take a local to notice the contrast in the quality of life between the city and the university; henceforth, in the context of a local's perspective, what were the key differences between the prestigious university and the simple city it was a part of, and why were these differences so prevalent today? What did it truly mean for an Earnestmore County local to attend a university right in their backyard?

On October 15, in an email interview with first-year student Tyler Johnson, member of the Wherewithal Football Team and Earnestmore County local, Johnson expressed his concerns with the cultural change he was exposed to in his first semester at Wherewithal. The initial underlying difference that set Wherewithal apart from the surrounding local schools was the rural roots students carried around with them. This rural background was evident in most students in the Earnestmore School District while emphasizing the importance of rural values in the community itself. Tyler was astonished to find that this "country or rural, almost badge of honor that most kids I grew up with felt they had to wear is not present [on campus]."

Needless to say, this coincided with the rural values Johnson was confident in being around while, in turn, also creating a political atmosphere he had never previously experienced. In Johnson's opinion, where most faculty, professors, students, and coaches "align themselves politically is in sharp contrast from North Earnestmore High School" and presumably Earnestmore County as a whole. Johnson did not shy away from revealing that due to this, and living off campus, he had not integrated into campus life in the fashion he had originally hoped for. Also seeing as how most of the student body Johnson had met were not from small towns themselves let alone anywhere near Earnestmore County, the "change of pace" and scenery that came with moving away from home was not a relatable subject in the eyes of Tyler, seeing as how he never left. Finally, Tyler could attest to the popular conjecture that Wherewithal was in a league of its own, atop a hill looking down on the city it was a part of. He also went on to say, the "wealth" associated with and at Wherewithal created a "bubble" separate from the folk who grew up around it. Ironically, while Earnestmore locals might be right down the street from the university, the prestigious life that ensued was a foreign concept to their overwhelming population. In 2019, the

United States Census Bureau reported that Earnestmore residents earned around $24,627 per capita, with 12 percent of the population stricken with poverty.

In another virtual interview conducted on October 21 via email, junior and Greendale local April Miller echoed a similar tone when communicating the difference in diversity and sense of community felt at Wherewithal. She also acknowledged the financial gap between families associated with students at Wherewithal versus the typical family living in Earnestmore County. April went on to further elaborate on the lack of diversity around her growing up by saying she had "grown up mostly around straight, white, conservative Christians" so it was "incredibly refreshing to come to Wherewithal and meet all kinds of different people with different backgrounds." Demographically speaking, she was right on the money: 91 percent of all citizens living in Sheetzville and Earnestmore County were white, and 68 percent of students at Wherewithal were white; all the while, the other third belonged to six major ethnic groups, including undocumented residents. She also mentioned the population of students at Wherewithal was "culturally, professionally, and stylistically more diverse" in comparison to the Greendale scene; in which case, it was very difficult to find people who didn't know one another through "professional/academic experiences" or people who fell outside of the conservative white demographic. A final and equally important point made by April was the resounding barrier students not from Earnestmore County cast, knowingly or unknowingly, that left locals attending Wherewithal feeling astray.

Class of 2020 graduate and gender studies major Megan Lease relayed the same message in an interview at Hops Brewing Company on October 20. She discussed her transition from Sheetzville Senior High School to Wherewithal University, in which she unregretfully admitted at the end of it all, she wished she had never gone to Wherewithal University. Interestingly enough, the reasoning behind such a claim wasn't due to the sudden change in politics as Tyler mentioned or even the widely prevalent financial gap between local students and Sheetzville newcomers. No, instead, it all tied back to her coming from Earnestmore County in the first place. "My dad was always around whenever I had a flat tire. I would go to bars and recognize everyone in the place. Everyone I grew up around was still there, and while it was nice, I was never truly on my own, and that's what matters. That's the college experience I wish I had looking back." To her, Sheetzville's twelve-mile radius felt claustrophobic, and although the university might be drastically different from Sheetzville, she felt as if she never branched outside of her small conservative town. During her first year, she said that she tried desperately to try and meet the status quo by dressing differently, acting differently, and presenting herself differently but then quickly realized there was no point to this at all. "I mean fuck that," she said, letting out a giggle while explaining that she was tired of being untrue to her identity. Even just after a few months, she was no longer willing to compete in the rat race that was and still is the social status ladder.

Tyler, April, and Megan all indicated that at one point or another, they had felt as if they were not as acclimated to life at Wherewithal as others despite being raised right in Earnestmore County. In fact, all three of them found Earnestmore County to be the very source of their struggles. Once again, all their responses were strikingly similar in nature. They found the lack of professionalism in the school corporation, lack of opportunities professionally, and lack of diversity to be the culprit of their misfortune that unfortunately seemed to follow a local student all four years. By not being exposed to new experiences, cultures, or opinions that pushed them out of their comfort zone, local students were deprived of the very attributes Wherewithal boasts about on a regular basis. Local students seemed to be at a severe disadvantage culturally, causing them to play catchup for the next several years upon arrival. While knowing the ins and outs of the university right down the road might seem fascinating, the truth was that it came at a steep price. Without the resources most other students had during their four-year development while in high school, Earnestmore County students were missing the fundamental parts of adolescence that created, defined, and molded future ambitions.

Journal 3

Just Out of Reach

Logging on to Zoom was usually something to dread. The fuzzy audio that cut in and out on a delayed signal made communication less than ideal. Instructors encouraged students to turn on their cameras, but nobody ever did. I felt inclined to turn on my camera since I knew no one else would. I did this for my professors' own sanity because I could only imagine how difficult it was to lecture twenty black boxes. This socially distant circus was enough to drive anyone mad, and it felt lonesome being the only one with my camera on, except in my COMM 200 level class. This class was different. This class had another student who strayed from the jaded narrative by also turning on their camera.

Laura Li was a bright, young, and vibrant girl who never missed a lecture, even the optional ones. The twenty-year-old's charisma was only overshadowed by the effort she willingly gave during class. Her astute attitude was always present for the 8:00 a.m. class, and from the moment she turned on her camera, revealing her lavishly tan skin complexion to her first of many intelligent proposals, I knew Laura was different. From what was visible within the limitations of the four-sided square screen, it was clear she was not on campus. The kitchen she streamed from had three windows perched above the cabinets that let in the eastern sunrise. The rays of light seemed to focus on her and nothing else. From time to time, I found myself pinning her video in favor of the PowerPoint, knowing this was the closest I could get to being in a classroom with actual people.

Her smooth, rounded, and porcelain face complemented her brown eyes and white teeth. She tied her dark hair in a bun, leaving a few strands poking out at the top. The black-and-gold Wherewithal sweatshirt she threw on before every meeting caused her hands to poke out ever so slightly while clutching a cup of coffee. Her soft-spoken voice alleviated the gray subject matter and was one of the only reasons I didn't fall asleep. A majority of what I knew about Laura stemmed from the first day of class when the professor sent us into breakout rooms with several other students to discuss our roots, interests, hobbies, and goals. Everyone's camera was off except hers and mine, so it felt as if it was just a conversation between the two of us. Laura wasted no time in starting the discussion.

"Hi, everyone, my name is Laura, and I am from Oklahoma City, Oklahoma. I am currently living in an apartment with some of my friends in Indianapolis for this semester." She continued by explaining her major in anthropology. "I choose anthropology because I just really love studying how other cultures interact with each other." With every passing second, Laura unveiled what her personality was, what her ambitions were, what made her happy, and what made her tick. However, these were not even the most revealing facets of her character. No, the subtle smirks she gave in between sentences and the frequent use of *um* as she thought of an articulate way to say she had a pet pig were all signs she was more than just a pretty face. Truth be told, this was worse than not knowing anything at all. She was already a captivating individual who was very attractive; but now knowing her inside out, it was troubling to realize we might never meet face-to-face.

She was a junior studying anthropology who played field hockey, so it was unlikely that we'd bump into one another let alone have another class together. The entirety of the situation was ironic. Laura and I saw one another on a weekly basis, but the barrier Zoom set between us was unsurpassable. Laura would never know who the other person with their camera on was. She would continue to be unaware that the person on the other end of the screen saw her in a light no one else did. Laura would attend every class with the same sweatshirt and cup of coffee in her hands, unaware of the elephant in the room while her roommates passed behind her looking aimlessly in the fridge for something they would never find.

Preserving Bygones in a World that Flies On By

It was apparent from his Albert E. Brumley "I'll Fly Away" ringtone that he was a man reminiscent of similar times. His thick prescription glasses rested atop his droopy ears that were similar to those of a basset hound. He had the voice of Disney's Goofy with a Southern twang and looked like the picturesque grandpa every grandkid imagined would read to them before bed. The pigment surrounding his cheeks and nose were naturally bright red. His grin stretched across the surface of his entire face. The fedora silhouetted under the desk lamp accented his buzz cut. His green suspenders latched onto his gray slacks while draping over his white button-up shirt. His black cotton-blend dress socks slipped into his shiny brown dress shoes. The smell of Clubman Pinaud powder radiated from his exterior. His working hands hinted at a long and intense physically demanding career. His friendly and hospitable nature spoke for itself. His name was Dave Richard. He was seventy years old and volunteered from one to four on Tuesday afternoons at the Earnestmore County Museum.

After trekking past the cracked and faulty parking lot, the lack of overall activity might deter someone from taking a tour, but upon further investigation, one would notice the stark contrast between the glowing faces seen at the counter and the unlit gallery behind them. Most days, staff spent the three hours the museum was open patiently waiting for someone to walk through the double-wide, translucent doors. As sad as it was, more times than not, their efforts were in vain.

"Since the pandemic, most afternoons here, we won't get a single visitor, and even then, it is usually one person that stops by very briefly to see her," he said, while pointing to the museum director's door.

These visitors were typically already involved with the museum and would stop by to ask questions concerning funds, new exhibits, or the museum's Facebook page. They came in passing, giving way for the sound of the air-conditioning kicking on and back off again that stood in place for what would normally be rehearsed tour guide banter. Brochures lay inside plastic holders engulfed with dust particles. The sheet of paper used to catalog the names of people who visited could be traced back weeks. Not a single book, picture, or knickknack was out of place at the gift shop, considering this was how the staff spent most of their time. Although despite the general lack of popularity for the museum at the moment, Dave Richard appeared to have a firm grip on his role as a docent chief editor of the newsletter and honorary board member for the Earnestmore County Museum.

Mr. Richard had several titles associated with his status at the museum; however, his start came only four years ago when searching for a place to store his newly deceased father's Army air corps dress uniform. Dave, having lived here his entire life, decided to donate the set to the museum.

"Hanging in my closet at home wasn't doing it any good," he explained.

After one thing led to another, Dave quickly found himself entangled inside the inner workings of the museum that was once a deserted Kroger grocery. As a docent, Dave was responsible for guiding and educating the public about the museum's pieces, but due to the current conditions involving COVID-19, "there is practically no traffic," he said with a frog in his throat.

He elaborated by explaining that the museum was actually only open by appointment; in which case, the lights were off unless a visitor happened to walk in. The thick novel on his desk next to the half-empty water bottle also pointed to the fact that once he sat down at his desk, it was a very rare occasion if he moved again except to leave. Prepandemic, it wasn't uncommon for Dave to give three or four tours to various groups of people in a single afternoon. Outside of his weekly commitment to the museum, the pandemic had not had a significant impact on his life.

"I live by myself."

He claimed the crop fields, cracked asphalt roads, and the ever-changing city known as Sheetzville as his forever home. However, he had never actually lived in the city itself, just the surrounding Earnestmore area. Dave was a retired diesel engine mechanic who previously worked for the Cummins engine distributor based out of Indianapolis. His job required that he drove days on end in and around Indiana, fixing, repairing, or installing heavy machinery. Having traveled across the farmlands, rolling plains, and lowlands Indiana was home to, he was not interested in leaving Earnestmore County. "I've done enough traveling for my job as it is," he said as he let out a subtle chuckle.

He continued to talk about his past, this time mentioning his family while he scratched the top of his head. "I've had two sons with my now estranged ex-wife, one of which passed due to health complications."

His only other extended family included his granddaughter, who was a kindergarten teacher, with whom his visits were seldom but sweet. In addition to being a proud father and grandfather, Dave's influences had changed as time had gone by.

After graduating from Sheetzville High School in 1968, Dave sought out to attend Rose Poly University, now known as Rose Hulman, to obtain an engineering degree. As luck would have it, following his first year, Dave decided to drop out altogether for a variety of reasons. "The Vietnam War was at its peak, and I was just as confused as everyone else," he said, shaking his head side to side.

When accounting for the given climate at the time, Dave was absolutely right. Confused was perhaps the very softest way of putting it. Dave was waving goodbye to his childhood and entering adulthood, while the world was collapsing around him. Civil rights protests, John F. Kennedy's assassination, and the Cuban Missile Crisis had all taken place beforehand. Of course, during his first year and a few months after he dropped out, Neil Armstrong landed on the moon, the My Lai massacre shocked the States, and all the while, the one place that seemed to stay the same was his hometown in Earnestmore County. Subsequently, Dave did exactly what he thought he needed to. He moved back to Earnestmore County and started a family three years later.

Dave said, "During this time, my only priorities were to feed my family and pay my bills." This, in turn, was what led him to work for Cummins Distribution Headquarters, but this job was also in line with what he would have liked to study at Rose Poly. Naturally, as time went on, his children grew older, his marriage withered out, and he finished his career as a mechanic; so Dave was in need of finding a higher purpose.

"If it wasn't for my father's passing, I may have never stumbled upon the museum and found my passion for historical research," he said, hunched over with his elbows resting on his knees. Needless to say, he had never left the area for an extended period of time, but he hadn't always been intrigued by preserving the town's history. When recollecting how he started out at the museum in the first place, Dave shared the cold reality some folks knew all too well.

"When you get older and you see all your older relatives start to go, there comes a day you look up and find you're the oldest one left," Richard said. When realizing this was indeed the unfortunate truth in his case, Dave knew he wanted to make the most of his time left. By preserving and writing about artifacts, paintings, souvenirs, and memorabilia, Dave hoped to inform and inspire future generations. Dave paused and stared at the white-tiled floor and said, "When I write, I write to look out for the little guy. I do this because I was once that young and ignorant little guy who had no clue what the world looked like before me, and I want to make sure the next generation has a sense of what the world was before they got here."

When on a tour through the museum with Dave, it did not take long to admire his passion for history. Dave hobbled from one exhibit to the next while gripping his brown wooden cane and said, "I'm still rehabbing my new knee so that's kinda consuming my time and my energy right now."

He wasted no effort in his telling of the exhibits. "This right here is the complete uniform set I mentioned earlier. The Army uniform was supported by a hanger that dangled from the smooth polished wooden coat rack it rested on. The navy-blue uniform was stiff from starch. It had golden stars on each end of the collar and was stitched together by the three bronze buttons that pop out around the midsection. The pants, bearing the same navy color were propped up behind the blazer. It was my father's, and luckily, the museum accepted it, so it will be here for quite some time," Richard said. When he spoke about his late father, his eyes gleamed, and he seemed to fall into some sort of blissful daydream. "Over here is a picture of one of the Earnestmore County railroad tracks my father took sometime around 1960, and if you look closely right below it, you'll see a picture I took in that exact same spot almost sixty years later," he said cheerfully, with his cane resting up against the door-frame. Each display in the museum had a story behind it, and Dave knew every person, place, and event coinciding along with them. From the antique green glass Coca-Cola bottles made in part from special sand only viable in Sheetzville to the shrines dedicated to the early prominent families in Earnestmore County, Dave was knowledgeable in every aspect imaginable.

Following what seemed to be an informative expedition into Earnestmore County's unique and fascinating history, Dave reflected on the town's developments over his lifetime. Reaching for the light switch, he expanded on the notion that while Sheetzville might not hold a candle to what it did forty years ago, Sheetzville had a special way of changing over the years. He clarified by reiterating the popular saying, "The more things change, the more they stay the same." In this moment, Dave left his role as a museum docent at the door, along with his cap and cane. He was no longer a friendly tour guide but a wise, lifelong citizen of Earnestmore County, opening up about his existential journey of living in Earnestmore County for seventy years.

Whistling with his lips in the shape of a scrunched *O*, he recalled how Earnestmore County looked and functioned in a way that was drastically different than now.

"When I was in school, IBM was going great guns, the zinc mill was very much still a viable operation, the railroads were all still running, and we even had regular bus service," Dave said. By and by time, raged on. It changed landscapes; it altered people and interests, and Dave had succumbed to the inescapable quintessence that was the ticking clock. Nevertheless, he preserved tiny pieces of Sheetzville to ensure the town's and his own legacy would live on long after he was gone.

Along with the vacancy of the museum came the vacancy of Richard's life and the town of Sheetzville. The way in which Richard envisioned his life was almost in direct correlation with the museum itself. Two parallel lines that had plummeted to the same desolate destination. The museum, a once popular upbeat area, had now turned to an empty, unfilled den of shadows. Meanwhile, Dave was on this island alone, surrounded by items that survived only through stories told by people like him.

"Dave would never say this, but in a lot of ways, he was the museum's saving grace," a voice said from the office kitty-corner to the gift shop. The museum director emerged. Her petite figure and stark black hair were in line with her gray pantsuit. She continued with her hands crossed, "Dave's timing was perfect. The museum desperately needed someone like him to take over the newsletter and take on a leading role here."

Dave reddened with embarrassment as the director retreated to continue filing papers. "I just do what I can and hope that at the end of the day it makes a difference," Dave said.

He did this through historical readings that happened to come across his desk at the museum or research conducted in his free time. At the ripe old age of seventy, Dave knew his days of working with his hands were long behind him. Consequently, he knew that whatever time he had left was best spent preserving the town he had never strayed from. His undying fidelity, fused with his spunky attitude, was captured in the museum's quarterly newsletters. In these newsletters, Dave covered the rugged and fascinating history in and around the Earnestmore County area. In one of his most recent articles "Ghost Towns and the Flood of 1875" published in January of

2019, Dave discussed the ghost town that was Pugville and how its geographical location made it a high-risk area for disasters, such as landslides and especially floods.

"Pugville was located in Washington Township, about a mile east of the Earnestmore-Cashen county line on the Old National Road. This would place it downstream of Reelsville along, or near Big Walnut." He continued by mentioning other landmarks in the surrounding area and even calling himself out later by wandering away from the topic at hand. "I mentioned the Flood of 1875 in the title, so I need to interrupt my story for a moment and talk about that flood." It was evident from this statement alone that Richard was utterly intrigued by the county's history, and his boy-like obsession over it only made him even more well suited for the job.

After volunteering for hours on end, Dave was greeted by his frigid car for a short ride back to his empty home located next to a field on the outskirts of town. He made dinner for one and reflected on his day of ambiguity as he searched for meaning in the smallest of things. His motives were to once again educate the everyday people of Sheetzville in the crowds he once lived for and to continue preserving Earnestmore's history one article at a time.

A Thank-You to My Aunt and Uncle

It was the summer of my senior year, and it was time to return to Rochester. Graduation was around the corner, and since the start of spring break, I was stuck in Texas finishing up the second semester of my senior year online. I knew staying with my grandmother was never an option. She was eighty-five, and I didn't want to risk exposing her, but besides that, she never would have let me out of the house once I got there. The South Bend local news had brainwashed her for months on end. She was a poor creature confined to her living room that entire year, but surprisingly enough, some part of her was okay with that. This was the same part of her that closed the blinds on sunny days and preferred to watch reruns of *The Price Is Right* as opposed to meeting up with her friends for coffee. She was never the same after my grandfather's passing, and when I was there, I did all I could, but just being there now wasn't even an option. I could not suffer the same fate as she and sacrifice my summer. It was the last time I would be around my friends before we set off for college to never return quite the same as when we left. It was in this state of confusion when my aunt and uncle invited me to stay with them over the summer.

To my uncle:

Your house was home to parties thrown for every occasion and all my failed summer romances. There was never any question about whom to go to for guidance or what time I needed to be home. Without you, I wouldn't know what sitting on a wave runner in the middle of a quiet lake feels like during dusk on a cool July evening. You let me be a reckless teenager and were always there to help clean up the mess. You laughed and watched from the balcony when I almost sank the pontoon while trying to fit eighteen people on it despite having a limit of ten. The fridge in the garage was always stocked with Trulys and Coronas so long as my friends and I were responsible. Your hot tub was perfect for nights when it was too cold to be out on the lake but my friends and I wanted to be outside.

You'd say, "Don't sweat it. She's not worth your time," when I'd get stood up after helping me set up the basement. Then said, "The basement is all yours," when they didn't. You helped me learn how to run a business firsthand and showed me the right decisions aren't always the easiest.

To my aunt:

Nothing would top the summer nights with the lake breeze blowing on our backs. The conversations held while sitting on the edge of the pier were timeless. It didn't matter what time or condition I arrived home in; you'd always insist on making me a hot meal. You would pull me out of bed on the days I'd sleep in until eleven and send me on a lunch run. You always kept matters interesting and were never afraid to let loose, especially during the Fourth of July. When going to get dinner across the lake, there was never a time you didn't invite me to tag along. There were also times before this when you tested my rite of passage, such as giving me the wheel at fifteen and trusting me to get everyone back home. Though perhaps my favorite time was when you lent me the electric-blue Dodge Charger for prom.

Without the two of you, my high school experience would have never been the same. You took me in as one of your own, and I'll appreciate that more than you'll ever know. There's no way to possibly repay all the favors you've given me over the last few years, but consider this a letter from me to you. That summer spent at your house will forever signify my efforts spent clinging onto the last bit of adolescence that was still within reach.

Shaving

Shaving is an essential step in anyone's adolescent youth. It is one of many transitional changes that each drag you a little closer to adulthood. And while it is a part of the awkward puberty bundle package that is voice cracks, acne, and body odor, it is something we all endure.

It was early June. I had been living with my aunt and uncle for a week and had just broken up with my girlfriend whom I'd been dating for a year and a half. I knew it would be hard enough to try and make things work from a distance, especially during my first year at college, so I decided to call it quits while we still had the summer to get over each other. Needless to say, she didn't agree with this rationale and proposed we could make it work if we both put in the effort. I disagreed. Not that I ever would have cheated on her while away, but the thought had crossed my mind, and I knew living with that guilt would have been exponentially worse than ending it then. It wasn't right, and in the end, she got punished for something completely out of her control. So naturally, I did the only thing an anxious eighteen-year-old boy fresh out of a long-term relationship would do. I Snapchatted almost every girl in my contacts. Most of them were smart enough to leave me on read, but it wasn't so much as me attempting to hook up with these girls as it was just craving companionship. I hadn't talked to most of these girls in months, and it was refreshing to speak with the ones who responded. This lasted for several days. Some evolved into regular flirtations while others remained completely platonic. However, the long and strenuous death that took hold of my summer would not come at the hands of one of these girls. Rather it came through an on-again, off-again high school crush who initially contacted me.

It didn't take long for the news surrounding my new relationship status to make it to every ear within a ten-mile radius. That's a small town for you. So when my high school crush Daisy B. reached out to me, I couldn't help to take the bait. I was eating cereal in the kitchen around 9:00 a.m. My aunt and uncle had left the house a while ago for work. I was looking for a job myself, and while my uncle could give me a day's work every now and then, it was never steady. At first, it was nice not having any responsibilities for a week or two after school ended, but after a while, it got to me. I started to feel like a bum with too much time on my hands, and the seldom days I did work for my uncle, he generously overpaid me. I needed something to kill time while also putting some money in my pocket for college. My friends all had summer jobs and were only available in the evenings after work, so for the first two weeks of summer, I was alone in my uncle's lakefront chalet. Poor me. Just as I finished my bowl of cereal, my phone buzzed twice. A Snapchat notification. Pulling my phone out of my pocket, I read the name under the Snapchat icon.

"Daisy B. is typing…"

"Daisy B has sent you a chat!"

I'll be damned. Before getting my hopes up, I thought it was probably just another standard, unoriginal message posing as a heartfelt response we modern teens knew all too well. Ah yes, probably just another "OMG, I heard the news. Are you okay?" or "Let me know if you want to talk."

To my surprise, it was quite the opposite. She didn't even acknowledge the breakup. I guess she assumed I already knew she was aware. Her snap read "Hey, IDK if you've got plans for tonight, but my friend Brooke, you know the one from Indy who plays on my travel softball team, is in town for the weekend and she's never been on a lake before, and I was wondering if you could take us out on the wave runner?"

I smirked and was feeling the best I had since the breakup. Those girls before were meaningless dead-ends. I and every girl I Snapchatted knew nothing tangible would reciprocate from these flirtatious texts, but they eased the isolation on both ends. I think

COVID-19 and the fact we would soon all be on our own in different corners of the country scared us senseless. I responded as fast as my thumbs could type.

"Are you kidding!? For sure. I'd love to. Let me just check with my aunt." She opened my Snap and replied immediately: "Okay, just LMK :)."

I couldn't believe my eyes. She could be the key to a great summer if tonight went well. Once my aunt gave me the okay, I confirmed it with Daisy B., who said they'd be over around seven. I eagerly watched as the hours flew by. It was now five, and my friend Bruce had just gotten off work. I called him to see if he would want to come over to prevent Brooke from having to third wheel. Bruce was also more or less fresh out of a relationship, so he was more than happy to oblige. He was over within the hour, and we couldn't help but converse about what could go down as we set up.

"Is Daisy's friend hot?" Bruce asked.

"I'm not sure, Bruce," I replied.

"You think she'll like me?" he asked.

"Bruce, I don't know. Just help me set up," I said while we made our way out to the dock. He sat on his response for a while then asked the million-dollar question.

"So what do you think will happen with you and Daisy tonight?" he asked while pulling off the cover to the wave runner.

"Uh, I'm not sure," I said. "I just hope we all have fun."

"Lame. I know what you really want," he said, now looking up at me smiling. "Don't even try to hide it. I know all about you two."

"Yeah, yeah, so we tried a few times in high school, and it didn't work. So what?" I asked mockingly.

"It means tonight's the night," he said, pulling two chairs to the end of the dock.

"Nah, man. You know I don't roll like that," I said, digging around in the speedboat for some towels.

"Yeah, okay. We'll see when they get here. You might be able to hide your excitement, but I know someone who can't," he said, thrusting his hips.

"Ew, Bruce, stop. Now come help me pick out some life jackets," I said, walking back toward the house. The girls were supposed to be here any minute. Once we got everything ready, Bruce and I finally had a minute to sit down in the basement and breathe. That one minute turned into five, then ten, then thirty minutes.

"You think they're coming?" Bruce asked.

"Chill, bro, they'll be here," I said reassuringly.

"Well, I'm not waiting on them," Bruce said, digging into the only kind of hors d'oeuvres I could afford. "You know these apple slices go really well with the caramel."

"I'm glad. Now save some for the girls," I said. Three-quarters of the snacks were gone by the time I got a text from Daisy B.

"Hey, we're here. Where do you want us to come in?"

"Through the back is fine," I replied. Moments later, out of the corner of my eye, I saw them walking around the side of the house toward the patio. Bruce and I almost tripped over each other trying to get to the door.

"Hey, glad you made it," I said.

"Yeah, it's good to see you," Daisy B. said, going in for a hug while Brooke and Bruce avoided looking at one another for too long.

"There are some snacks inside if you guys are interested," I said.

"I think we're good, actually. Brooke and I just had dinner. Where should we get changed?" Daisy said, holding up her black bikini.

"Just inside to the right, you'll see a bathroom," I replied.

"Okay, we'll be out in a few," she said as she shut the glass door behind them.

"Did you see Brooke?" Bruce asked, turning around to get one last glimpse.

"Yeah, why?"

"I want her—bad," Bruce said.

"Well, whatever you do, don't let her see the drool on the side of your lips when she gets back out here."

"Oh, shut up, man!" Bruce said, punching me in the arm.

The girls were back out in no time and looked absolutely stunning. I gulped the same way a cartoon character would do when they'd bitten off more than they could chew.

"What are we doing just standing here? Let's go," Daisy B. said, giggling and pushing past Bruce and me.

"You and Brooke wait here. I'm going to take her out," I said, leaning in toward Bruce.

"What do you expect me to do with her?" Bruce asked nervously.

"I don't know? Talk," I said, shrugging and walking backward. Daisy had already found a life jacket and was waiting at the end of the pier for me. I lowered the wave runner into the water and told her to hop on. She jumped on and put her hands around my waist. We took off and never looked back. The wind played with her golden hair as we skimmed across the lake. She clung to my life jacket when I topped it out at sixty-two and then rested her chin on my shoulder when I brought it back down. I cut the gas, and we gazed at the sunset without saying a word. I could have stayed there for hours until she pulled me out of the trance when she spoke.

"Don't you think we should head back before it gets too dark? Brooke and Bruce haven't got a turn yet."

"Yeah, definitely," I said, starting the engine. We had only been out there for twenty minutes, but when I was with her, time seemed to stand still. We understood each other, respected one another, and had always had history. From the day when I was just the new kid, up until now, Daisy and I had always bonded. We'd get in trouble when we'd laugh too loud in study hall or when she attempted to draw Texas in our World Literature class. It was rare to find a girl I had this strong of a connection with at my previous school of three thousand students, let alone Rochester Community High with four hundred. She was special, but she also had her demons. We arrived back at my uncle's house with fifteen minutes of daylight left, and from the looks of it, Bruce and Brooke were having a grand time while we were away. They kept chatting until they got to us.

"Finally. What were you guys doing out there?" Bruce asked, fastening his life jacket.

"It's been twenty minutes, Bruce, relax," Daisy said. I always admired how she could stand up to anyone, particularly men. Brooke and Bruce hopped on and didn't say a word. "Don't kill her, Bruce," Daisy yelled as they left the no-wake zone. She sighed and sat down in one of the two chairs at the end of the pier. "Aren't you gonna sit down? They won't be back for a while," she said.

"Well, duh," I replied playfully.

"Thanks for having us over. It really means a lot to us, to me," she said, correcting herself.

"Of course, it's no problem, really," I said, looking back at her. She sat with her legs crossed and her arms resting on the sides of the chair. Her blue eyes pierced my inner thoughts. She knew what I was feeling but wouldn't act on it until later. After all, it was rumored that she and an old flame were talking again. This old flame happened to be one of my close friends, and I never was one to overstep my boundaries. "So I gotta ask, are you and Luke talking?"

"Ugh, no. I don't know why everyone thinks that. We had our time, and it didn't work," she said, putting her hair to one side.

"Well, that's what I'm hearing," I interjected.

"Actually, he got mad I was even coming over here tonight. You wanna see?" she said, retrieving her phone. "Look."

"I think BJ likes you, and honestly, I'm kinda jealous."

"See," she said, pulling her phone away. "He may think we're something, but I can assure you we're not." While it was a relief to see that, I still didn't want to step on Luke's toes. They had dated senior year, but it didn't take an insider to see Luke was putting in 95 percent of the effort. He was the one who posted about her on social media, and he was the one who bought her gifts, not vice versa. Luke was a genuinely nice guy; for him, dating her was an honor. For her, it looked like their relationship was just something to keep her entertained. Before matters got too personal, I made small talk until Brooke and Bruce made it back. Sure enough, they did. Brooke was soaking wet, and Bruce was laughing hysterically.

"You should have seen how far she flew off," Bruce said in between laughs.

"Oh my gosh, are you okay? Sorry, he's kind of a show-off," I said.

"I'm fine. It was so much fun," she replied.

"You know, the point of driving a wave runner isn't to throw the other person off. That's what tubing is for," I said, crossing my arms.

"I'm so glad that wasn't me," Daisy B. said, helping Brooke off. "I would've killed him."

"She said she was fine, didn't she?" Bruce said rhetorically. He raised the wave runner while I got the girls' towels. The sun had set, and it was getting chilly. Daisy spoke for the two of them when she said they were going to get changed again. Shortly after that, we said our goodbyes and they left. Bruce couldn't contain himself.

"I think I'm in love," he said once we got inside.

"You cannot be serious, dude," I said, throwing away the dried-up brown apple slices.

"I am, though. She is perfect."

"How so?" I asked.

"We just have so much in common, and I've never met anyone like her," Bruce said with his feet up on the table. "We're gonna have to find a way to get them back here."

"Easy there, bachelor, you don't even know if she feels the same," I said, putting away my life jacket.

"Oh, she will. I just gotta give her some time," he said, now leaning forward. "And you gotta work your magic to get them back here."

"First of all, she reached out to me. Second, I'm sure they'll want to come back at some point. And lastly, we'll see what happens," I said. We each talked about our separate nights for the next hour before Bruce decided it was time to go home. I showed him out then made my way to my room. After taking a shower and brushing my teeth, I got in bed. It was too early to go to sleep, so I turned on the television and watched *Rick and Morty*. Halfway through the first episode, my phone buzzed. I hadn't been on it all day and presumed it was someone sending me a black screen with the words "gn streaks" on it. To my surprise, for the second time that day, it was no other than Daisy B. I swiped over and read.

"Thanks again for having us over. I had a great time." Could this be happening? Did she like me? What do I do now? I responded with a generic message.

"You're welcome. I had fun too." It was nothing crazy, but then again, I was just testing the waters. It wasn't long before she replied and left no room for interpretation.

"I know I wasn't the only one who felt something at the end of the pier tonight. I could see the way you looked at me." Butterflies went wild in my stomach. I was done playing coy now and responded with a message of my own.

"Is that so? Who could blame me if I was?" I was never the best at flirting. She paused and left me on read for a few minutes then sent another snap. It was a game.

"Does BJ have a crush on me?"

"I mean, I don't know if I'd go that far," I replied lightheartedly.

"Well, if you did, what do you find so fascinating about me?"

"Well, I wouldn't know where to start, honestly. There's that rare smile you only show to a select number of people, you relate to me like no other person I know, you're not afraid to get deep with me, and when you're around, I feel like we can both just be ourselves." Her Bitmoji popped in the chat as soon as I hit send. Seconds later, the thought bubble appeared above its head, and she responded.

"Awww, that means a lot coming from you. I feel the same way."

I wasn't looking for a relationship, but when she said that, I couldn't help to imagine what one would look like between us. She was beautifully seductive, and even after all these years, the only thing we had ever done was hug. We were one and the same. Even my friends said they could see us dating. And if that wasn't enough, my mom had met her several times at football games and my birthday parties throughout the years. It wasn't an exaggeration to say my mom might have liked Daisy B. more than I did, but that was because my mom saw everything I did. Then again, I also saw more than my mom did, and if we were going to start something, I needed to know everything. It was impossible to build something meaningful if the very foundation of what supported it were lies. Rumors had followed her throughout high school, and she had a reputation of being a tease, so before we started anything, I needed to know she had grown out of that. I got straight to the point with my next snap.

"Okay, but if we're gonna do this, just know I have my reservations."

"What kind of reservations?" she asked.

"Well, it's no secret we tried time and time again only to have it blow up in my face every time, so what makes it any different this time?"

"I'm not even the same person anymore, BJ. I was immature and stupid back then." It was difficult to ask the next question, but it needed to be done.

"Okay, then that solves the first problem, but besides hearing you were talking to Luke again, I heard you were thinking about batting for the other team."

"Are you serious? Who did you hear that from?"

"Daisy, I've heard it from a bunch of people, not just one."

"It's not true. God, I hate when people gossip about me. They don't even know me."

"Hey, I never said it was. I just needed to know that it wasn't."

"Okay, well now you know." She used the excuse that she needed to go to bed, but I could tell she just didn't feel like texting anymore, which was fair. At the same time, some of these rumors had been around since junior year, and I found them strange because it seemed like she was always talking to some guy at our school. I told her good night and ended every streak I had with the other girls before dozing off. If she was going to fully commit, it was only right I did the same.

I woke up the next morning around ten thirty and hoped to see a text from Daisy. I was wrong in doing so. My phone was dry. I reached out to her first and sent her a good morning text. It wasn't until 1:00 p.m. she responded.

"Hey," I replied a couple of minutes later.

"What's up?"

"Nothing really." This was going nowhere. Struggling to keep the conversation alive, I took a shot in the dark.

"If this is about last night, I apologize. I know they are just rumors, but I had to know."

"It's okay, but can we just not talk about that anymore?"

"Of course, I'm sorry."

"Okay, I have to go now, but we can talk later." I was relieved to be out of the doghouse but curious as to what I was going to do with the rest of my day. I needed a job. My friend Edward worked for a construction company based in town and mentioned they might need an extra set of hands, so I met up with him after he got off.

Pouring a glass of Crystal Light, he asked why I came over.

"Can't two friends just hang out?" I asked.

"I'm tired and sweaty. I know you wouldn't have come over here right after I got off work unless you wanted something. So what is it?" he asked, standing in his lime long-sleeve shirt speckled with paint.

"I need a job," I said, sitting on his couch.

"What about the television station?" he asked.

"That was more of an internship for school. I need something full time," I responded. "What if I worked with you?"

Peering in through the kitchen, he looked surprised. "I don't know if we still need an extra guy, but I can check. Is that all you came over here for?"

"That and to hang out with you, why?" I asked.

"All right, put on a movie or something, and I'll text Michael," he said, washing out his cup.

"Michael? As in Daisy's older brother?" I asked.

"Yeah. You know I always thought you and her would make a good couple," he said.

"So I've heard," I said, scrolling through his gallery of movies. I heard a chime, and then Edward informed me of his boss's response.

"You're in. Can you start tomorrow?"

"Sure thing, what time?" I asked.

"It's 6:00 a.m., and don't wear anything nice. Now put on *Mad Max: Fury Road*. The cinematography is unreal," he said. We finished the movie, and I went home for the night. I sat down for dinner and texted Daisy the good news.

"Guess who starts working for your brother tomorrow?"

"Ooo, someone's finally employed?" she responded.

"Oh shut up, LOL. That means I'll be seeing more of you, ya know."

"I know. I'm happy for you. Good luck. I know you guys start early, so I'll let you get some rest."

"Thanks, I'll see you tomorrow. Good night."

"Night," she texted back. We did start early that next morning and most weekday mornings after that. I would watch the sunrise on our way to a worksite and watch it set as the crew and I finished painting or, as the experienced call it, striping the parking lots. It was tough and sometimes grueling work, but anything the crew did, Michael was there right alongside us. On the days we would get rained out, he made sure to pay us for the trip there and back. He was a good boss but an even better man. I admired his attitude and hoped to run a business similar to his image after college. I was almost positive he knew about his sister and me, but that was a conversation I never wanted to address, especially at work. And despite starting and ending every day at their house, I never saw much of Daisy. It wasn't above Edward to go into their house and pester Daisy in the mornings, but I never joined in while on company time. That and I didn't want Michael to get the wrong impression of me. This restricted my interactions with Daisy to mostly over the phone. We were both busy during the week, and the weekends weren't much better. Softball tournaments across the state claimed most Saturdays and Sundays, and when I wasn't picking up a shift for her brother, I did my best to make it to every tournament. Her parents were well aware of my efforts, and we'd casually say hello when we'd bump into each other at these events. The thing is, I don't think Daisy B. ever realized she had an entire support system behind her, and it never seemed to bother her that we didn't get to hang out alone. It felt as if me showing up to these events was enough for her.

The first half of summer followed this repetitive cycle. I'd work Monday through Friday then travel to another city to go watch her play. It was now mid-July, and summer was quickly slipping through our hands. We still hadn't been on a date by ourselves, and it started to get to me. When I would try and make plans, she always claimed to be working or practicing for softball. I wouldn't let this red flag sit for long. I texted her that we needed to have a heart-to-heart and decide if she wanted to make this work, to which she regretfully conceded to come over. This was the first time she had come over alone all summer.

"All right, I'm here. What did you want to talk about?" she asked as we walked down to the basement.

"Daisy, doesn't it bother you we haven't been on a single date yet?" I asked, sitting down and ushering her to do the same.

"We've both been busy, BJ. What do you want me to do?" she said, finding a seat.

"That may be true, but take a look at where we're at. The first half of summer is gone, and we have nothing to show for it," I said.

"That's not true, BJ. We've done so much together," she said.

"Like what?" I asked with my elbows resting on my knees in a hunched position.

"Well, you've been to my softball games, we went out on the lake again, and you brought me Sprite while I was at work," she said, sitting back.

"Are you serious? I came to your softball games because it's the closest thing there is to us being together. I took you and your friends out on the lake on one of my only days off and didn't get so much as a hug. And yeah, I brought you a Sprite when I got off work on my way home. How is that anything close to us being together?"

"I don't know what to tell you. I've been busy, and I want to hang out just as much as you." She was a broken record spitting out the same lies over and over again. I was infuriated. The only thing I could think of was a quote my mom had told me.

"You make time for the people you care about. You make excuses for the ones you don't." She went to speak but hesitated and, instead, let out a half-baked sigh.

"Look, I'm having a bonfire this Saturday. I'd love it if you came. I know I haven't been the best at communicating lately, but you need to understand my situation."

"No, what I think needs to happen is we need to decide if we're going to be friends or something more," I fired back.

"What do you want?" she asked.

"You've known from day one I've wanted to make this work, but you're not making it very easy. I think we need to take a step back and just be friends."

"Wow, okay," she said with an awkward laugh as she looked at the ground and put her hair behind her ear. "I didn't expect that from you, but if it's what you think's best, then okay." I walked over to the steps leading up to the door and turned around. "So no hug then," she said. I was lost. She was an impossible enigma that could never be satisfied. I leaned in and gave her a side hug so she wouldn't have anything to complain about. As she went through the front door, she turned around and asked, "Are you coming to my bonfire then? Bruce can come too."

"Yeah, I'll be there," I said. I was only going for Bruce, really. He was still utterly obsessed with Brooke, and I knew he wouldn't have passed at another opportunity to slide. There was radio silence between the two of us for the rest of that week. I had seen her in passing at the start of each day as I loaded traffic cones into her brother Michael's truck, but neither one of us would try to start a conversation with the other outside of a friendly wave. Most of the time, she would still be in her polyester pajamas, bleary-eyed and barefoot, yet she still looked as beautiful as she did on the dock. There was never going to be an easy way out of our doomed romance. It was dead on arrival. Even if I had known what was to come, I was much too stubborn and she, too gorgeous to pull out now. There was only one destination for our relationship's inevitable demise, and that was to end in flames.

Saturday night was here, and Bruce was even more upbeat than his usual self. I picked him up, and on his way to my car, I saw him cradling four shirts as he passed my headlights. He got inside and didn't say anything. All he had was a huge grin on the side of his face, and I immediately interjected.

"Okay, I'll bite. What's with all the T-shirts?"

"You should know me well enough by now to know what those are for," he said, reclining the passenger seat.

"Surely you can't go through five shirts in one night, can you?" I asked.

"I can't help that I get nervous, and yes, yes, I can," he said. Of course, we were referring to the profuse amount of sweat that radiated from his skin. It was an egregious amount, really, and I had seen him go through a shirt or two during a workout but never five in one night. *I guess he's just being extra cautious,* I thought, as I built a queue of songs for the trip to Daisy's house. We shouted and sang the whole way there, trying to hype ourselves up, but deep down, I think we were both anxious for different reasons. He was trying to shoot his shot with a girl out of his league that wasn't feeling him to begin with, and I knew no matter how hard I tried there was going to be an awkward encounter or two. Everyone was either in lawn chairs next to the fire or playing speed pong by the garage. I parked off to the side of her house knowing I might have to leave quickly if the night aged poorly, but soon, leaving at all wasn't an option. There were cars backed up to the tree line that bordered the road. I expected ten or fifteen people at the most, but this was Daisy's party, I should've known better. Before long, it seemed as if every socioeconomic group Rochester catered toward was there. It didn't matter who was invited so long as there was a sea of bodies. Lake house residents, trailer park occupants, city slickers, and country mavericks all fraternized with each other. For the first hour, Daisy B. was nowhere to be seen. Bruce and I grabbed one of the few remaining lawn chairs and sat by the fire so we could discuss a game plan.

"Bro, how am I going to get close to Brooke? She's playing pong and is surrounded by thirty people," Bruce said.

"Relax, Bruce, I can't even find Daisy," I said, putting a drink under my chair.

"I thought you and her were through?" he asked.

"As much as I'd like to be, it's not that easy," I replied.

"What did she do this time?" he asked, taking a sip.

"Actually, nothing. She accepted I just wanted to be friends, but when I saw her a couple days ago in her pj's—I can't describe it to you—I didn't know how to feel. I don't want this summer to go to waste, and I sure as hell don't want to be sitting back a few months from now wondering, what if? It's only a few weeks before we venture out and discover new people. I can't throw away my only shot," I said, looking into the fire.

"Well, sounds like you got some things to sort out. I'm going to try and see if Brooke wants to play cornhole. I think she just finished her game of pong, and the crowd is dying down," he said, getting up and throwing his can into the fire. I moved my chair and meshed with a group of high school acquaintances as I looked over my shoulder every few minutes, searching for Daisy. Several dull conversations later, I heard "Mr. Brightside" playing on the other side of the bonfire. I grabbed my chair and wandered across the wet grass to find Daisy with a speaker at her feet surrounded by an entourage of guys who she called friends. Some of them were in college already, and the others I knew from school. She encouraged me to have a seat next to her, and I did. The look on these guys' faces spelled murder. They genuinely looked jealous, and for the life of me, I couldn't figure out why. *Was she entertaining multiple guys? Had she been leading them on too?* I had no idea nor time to theorize. I had decided to enjoy the night for what it was, and I did. We shared a few laughs and loosened up with one another as the hours went by. By the time I bumped into Bruce again, he was on his fourth shirt and couldn't hit the side of a barn in cornhole. He was mellow and draped over Brooke while he threw his bag. Normally, she wouldn't have entertained him, but she was feeling a bit woozy herself. Daisy called the next game of cornhole while I found us a couple of chairs to sit down and watch. Upon doing so, I found two empty lawn chairs next to the garage; however, they were also right next to the smoke circle. In an attempt to retrieve the chairs, I swiftly walked over to where they were propped up against the garage and grabbed them. When I turned around, I heard someone shout my name. It was Grace, Daisy's best friend at the time.

"BJ, come sit over here for a sec," she said as she took a rip. She was a college sophomore who transferred from IU and hadn't been the same since she peaked in high school.

"I was just grabbing these two chairs," I replied as I kept walking.

"Just for a sec. I need to ask you something," she said waving me over. There was a thin cloud of secondhand smoke surrounding her. The smell of her THC cartridge wafted my way and only grew stronger as I dragged the two chairs behind me, scuffing the bottoms of them on the concrete along the way.

"What's up?" I asked.

"Oh, nothing. I hope you've been treating Daisy right," she said, taking another hit.

"I always have," I said questioningly.

"I saw her showing you off tonight. She doesn't do that for just any guy, ya know?" she said, exhaling.

"I'm aware," I replied.

"I mean, you guys are still talking, right?" she asked.

"It's complicated," I replied.

"What do you mean? You either are or you're not," she said. "So what is it?"

"Yes, yes, we're talking. Now will you drop the game of twenty questions?" I asked.

"Good," she said. "I'm happy for you guys." Just as Grace finished speaking, I saw Daisy standing behind me. She smiled and didn't say anything. She just sat down next to me while Grace gave us some space.

"Lean in next to me," Daisy said. "I want to take a picture." I leaned in, and she stuck her tongue out as she took the picture. In that moment, I was starstruck. Perhaps our summer was still salvageable after all. "So are we going to go play cornhole?" she asked.

"Uh, yeah. Let's go," I replied, getting up. What started as one game turned to best of three, then best of five, and finally, best of seven. Daisy refused to lose, and that was the case for most things. She was determined to have it all and nothing less. After we won the series four to three, the party had withered out significantly. I helped Daisy put away the cornhole boards in the garage, and she started conversation.

"You came in clutch that last game," she said, setting one of the boards on top of a self.

"You're the one who scored the final point," I said, chuckling and shaking my head.

"It was easy. By the way, did you see Luke leave?" she asked.

"Uh, no. Now that you mention it, I didn't notice he was even here," I said, handing her the other board.

"I think he left early because he got mad," she said.

"At what?" I asked. "Me?"

"I think so," she said as we walked out of the garage.

"I don't understand. I thought you told him how you felt?" I asked.

"I did! I guess he still thinks he's got a shot," she said, closing the garage door.

"Well, you can't satisfy everyone, Daisy. Some people just aren't going to see it the same as you," I said. I defended her time after time even when I shouldn't have.

"Yeah, I guess you're right. Do you want to come inside and play cards? I have a few friends who are spending the night," she said.

"Sure," I said, looking back. My car was still blocked in, and I had nowhere to be. When we got inside, a few of her friends had already called it a night and were asleep in her bed. Bruce was nowhere to be found, but on my way inside, I noticed the sweaty shirts he had gone through were still inside my car. We sat at the long rectangular table inside of her den and waited for her friends to join us from outside. Edward came crashing in and sat down next to me. He had spent the night alongside Michael and the other coworkers. Grace then came inside, along with Daisy's softball friends. We played blackjack for the next thirty minutes until Bruce came stumbling in and informed all of us of his night with Brooke.

"ThAt WaS tHe BeSt NiGhT oF mY LiFe," he said, slurring his words.

"What did you do to Brooke?" Daisy asked, folding her cards.

"nOtHiNg. ALL wE dId WaS pLaY cOrNhOle ThEn I mAsaGed HeR LEg UnTiL sHe feLL AslEEp," he said, finding a chair. That would be the furthest he ever got with her, too, because she woke up the next morning absolutely mortified. We played cards until 4:00 a.m., and Daisy insisted I spend the night rather than driving home that late. So Bruce and I slept in the basement while she and her friends slept in her room upstairs. It took an eighteen-point turn to get out that next morning, but Bruce and I were both pleased at how the night unfolded. The last four weeks of summer looked as promising as ever.

Another week and a half had gone by since the party. Work started to get busier, but I didn't mind. Edward and I would sweat for hours on end in the July heat and bonded during lunch breaks when we'd eat takeout off Michael's tailgate. As for Daisy B. and I, we agreed we were too passionate about each other to just stay friends. We texted more and communicated better. Since the party, I had been to another one of her tournaments and even played sand volleyball with her and her friends at the park. It was nice spending more time with her, yet we still had not been on a single date yet. That same red flag from before had now grown into an inhibition and wasn't going away. I called her that night to express my concerns, with hopes to schedule a date.

"Hello," she said, picking up the phone.

"Hey, Daisy."

"Hey, what's up?" she said.

"I don't know about you, but since the party, I feel like we've only gotten closer. I've enjoyed every minute together, but don't you think it's time we go on a date? Ya know, just the two of us?" I asked, pacing across my bedroom floor.

"BJ, you know I love hanging out with you, and yes, I do feel like we've gotten closer since my party. I can't promise that we'll get to go on a ton of dates before the summer ends, but yes, I agree." *It's about time,* I thought. The six-week saga that was chock-full of misery and confusion was at its end.

"Okay, great. I'm off this Thursday, if that works for you," I said, sitting on my bed.

"I think I'm free then, too, actually," she said.

"How's eight sound?" I asked. "My place?"

"I'll be there," she said intimately.

"I can pick you up if you'd like," I said.

"No, no, it's fine. I'll meet you there," she said, trying not to put me out. We said our goodbyes, and I was the happiest I'd been since the party. I busted my tail at every jobsite that week to ensure Thursday remained open. It was going to be perfect; it had to be.

Three back-breaking and sun-stricken days later, it had arrived. My uncle spent that evening helping me prep the basement and even found a rom-com about a softball player on Netflix for us to watch.

"The basement is yours," he said, when we finished cleaning and setting up the surround sound speakers.

"Thanks again," I said, laying out a few blankets.

"Don't mention it. It's what I'm here for," he said, heading back upstairs. It was only five thirty, and I was beat. I fell asleep on the couch before I could even set an alarm. When I awoke, it was seven thirty, and I still hadn't heard from Daisy. Ergo, I snapped her to make sure we were still on.

I sent a picture saying, "Hey, looking forward to seeing you soon :)." She responded fifteen minutes later.

"Me too. Can't wait." This was actually happening. I went upstairs, brushed my teeth, and combed my hair to make sure that nap didn't set me back too much. When I checked my phone again, it was 8:00 p.m. *I'm sure she's right around the corner,* I thought. Soon, it was 8:15 p.m. but still no sign of Daisy. At 8:20 p.m., I sent a snap asking if something had come up. Still no reply. At nine, I turned off the TV downstairs and moped up to my bedroom. My feet weighed fifty pounds, and my throat swelled shut. Leading me on was one thing. Standing me up was another. Now that my night was spoiled, I had nothing to do except go to sleep. My eyes watered to compensate for the anger coursing through me as I rolled over in bed. Dozing off, I heard my phone buzz. *I wonder who that could be?* It was 9:45 p.m., and the only excuse that could have rescued her at that point was if she had gotten in a car accident, God forbid. I left her on delivered until ten and then opened her message.

"Hey, I'm on my way over," she typed.

"You're a joke," I replied back.

"What?"

"You don't see a single thing wrong with what you just pulled, do you?" I asked.

"I mean, I'm still coming. What's the big deal?" she asked, oblivious of her wrongdoings.

"Daisy, it's ten o'clock. My aunt and uncle are asleep. They have work in the morning, and so do I," I texted.

"BJ, I was out with some friends, and we got some ice cream. You're overreacting." She insisted. I was in total disbelief. I had never encountered someone so narcissistic or delusional. I left her on read and double-checked that my 6:00 a.m. alarm was set for tomorrow morning. When I woke up, I had zero notifications waiting for me. Daisy B. was never one to double text. It would have hurt her pride too much. She and I both knew this was the end. Except, our summer story wouldn't end there. No, this ugly monstrosity and sorry excuse for a summer fling could only end in dramatic fashion. When I got off work that night, I got a call. Not from Daisy B, not from my aunt or uncle, and certainly not from any of the girls I previously Snapchatted. It was from no other than my ex-girlfriend, Jennifer, and she wasted no time cutting to the chase.

"Are you talking to Daisy?" she asked as soon as I answered.

"No," I said, not knowing how much she knew.

"Well, I hope you know what you're doing because you're going to get hurt again," she said, seeing straight through my lie. I didn't know what to think. My head spun with motives for her to reach out to me.

"Look, if this is some warning, I don't want it. I know what I'm doing," I said, trying to remain headstrong.

"I'm going to make this quick. You might want to check your girl because someone texted me, and they're not happy. I think she's been unfaithful," she said.

"If you're talking about Luke, then save it. I already knew about them, and we didn't do anything anyway," I said, giving up the charade.

"Um, no. Not him. Like I said, ask your girl. I just want what's best for you, and I don't think she's been honest with you," she said, hanging up the phone. I wanted to believe she did want what was best for me, but I couldn't help to think she was just interfering. I texted Daisy to confront her, but unsurprisingly, she played coy as well. With a little digging and help from Edward and Bruce, we discovered Daisy had been entertaining Luke and a girl from the next town over. Turns out, this girl was the one who reached out to Jennifer because she knew we had dated and was suspicious of Daisy. It all clicked. Daisy had not only created a love triangle but a bisexual love square. The rumors, the lies, and the excuses, it all made sense. She was seeing this girl and Luke on the days she'd be too busy to see me, but when she needed to make a public appearance, I was her crutch. I was the beard covering her true identity, and it was time to cut her off once and for all. The only problem with this—my father never taught me how to shave.

Although he did often mention a rather outdated saying by today's terms, which was "Girls are like cars. The prettiest are often the hardest to maintain." And as sexist as it was, I'll be damned if it wasn't true. The saddest part of it all, she was my first crush, and it might have actually worked if our entanglement wasn't unrequited.

While most people might have cursed her out, I handled it the only way I knew how, with class. Rather than spread rumors or tell her family, I took away her only gift of hope. I enlightened Luke of his situation and informed him of the role he was playing in her game of Go Fish. I came to find out he had no idea of this affair either, but he and I would joke about it in passing for weeks to come. She had been feeding him the same lines she fed me. As for the mystery girl, she was content with being Daisy's dirty little secret. I never did see her that summer, and for all I know, she could have had a beard too.

In the aftermath, I made sure to thank Jennifer. She did have my best interests at heart, along with the courage to call me out on my BS. She was single-handedly the best thing to ever happen to me, and it's true when they say, "You never know what you really have until it's gone."

I then later learned Daisy tried to have me fired once I found out, most likely out of fear that I would mention something to Michael. Although something tells me he wasn't too fond of this idea because he invited me to come back and do it all again next summer.

Journal 4

Easy Like a Sunday Morning

My eyes opened as the sunlight poured in through the white voile sheers. I picked my head up off the pillow and faced the milky walls that were covered with sporty action shots of my friends and me. It was 9:32 a.m., and church started in an hour and a half. I folded my comforter on top of itself, revealing my legs and torso. I placed my feet on the numbingly cold wooden floor, stood up, and avoided every creak in the floor so as not to wake my grandmother, who was only a few doors down. I made my way to the closet and ran my fingers across the plastic hangers, still trying to decide what to wear. I passed on wearing the letterman I had worn the last two days in a row in favor of a cream polo cardigan. Most kids wore a T-shirt and basketball shorts to the service, but I had always been taught to dress up on the Lord's day. Contemplating what pair of slacks to wear was a no-brainer. I only had the one pair of gray Calvin Klein dress pants that were worn and washed once a week for this reason and this reason only. I then slipped on my Kenneth Cole penny loafers and placed my hand on the golden doorknob.

I opened the cedar door that was chipping away at the bottom as I wondered what I was going to have for breakfast. I knew my grandmother had just been to the grocery store, so my options were arguably limitless. There was no rush to put down a bowl of cereal like there was on weekdays. I had the time, and I intended to use every minute of it. I reached inside of the lazy Susan and spun it 180 degrees to where the toaster was hidden. I plugged the toaster into the outlet under the cupboard and then opened the freezer. Waffles would be my meal choice that morning. I sinfully indulged in the first two chocolate chip waffles alone with an unhealthy amount of Pearl Milling Company maple syrup. As I pressed down on the front switch of the toaster, the insides glowed a fluorescent orange. Forty-five seconds later, the second batch of waffles sprang from the depths of the toaster, gasping for cool air. I daintily placed them on my paper plate to avoid getting burned as my grandmother walked in.

"What are you making?" my grandmother questioned.

"I am just making some waffles." I insisted.

"How many have you had? You better not be pigging out on those," she barked. I ignored her last comment and continued to soak my waffles in syrup. I then sat down at the kitchen table and watched as my grandmother struggled to turn on her twelve-inch box television that was perched in the corner across from the table. The static spread across the screen as she successfully turned on the television. It made a high-frequency ringing noise as it found its way to the Fox News network. We sat in silence as she slurped on her first cup of coffee—black. My waffles were now gone, and it was time to freshen up. I crumpled up my paper plate, still dripping with syrup, and placed it in the trash. Before I could turn on the faucet, my grandmother yelled.

"You know you are not supposed to wash your hands in my kitchen sink! What in God's name are you doing?"

"Yes, ma'am. I do not know what I was thinking." The hysteria, the virus, and the pure isolation turned her heart cold. She wouldn't stay like this forever, but it was difficult to see her this way for so long. Later down the road, when I'd visit from college, she'd practically collapse from glee, but it was safe to say we all had different ways of coping. I then marched to my bathroom, where I washed the sticky residue off my fingers. I brushed my teeth and rinsed my mouth out with the city pipeline water that tasted of iron and fluoride. Lastly, two spritzes of Acqua di Gio cologne for good measure. I placed the cologne back inside of the mirrored cabinet and pressed it shut, leaving behind a thumbprint I knew I would have to clean off later. I licked the tip of my index finger and pressed down the one Alfalfa hair sticking up from the back of my cowlick, and it was time to leave. My grandmother stood with her arms behind her back, peering out of the back door, as I grabbed my car keys. I unlocked both locks on the front door and stopped at the screen. Just before closing the door, I pleaded.

"Bye, Grandma, I am going to church. I love you."

"Okay, I will see you when you get back," she mumbled. She hated when I left the house. All she longed for was companionship but had a hard time expressing this.

My car did not want to turn over at first, but sure enough, it did; it always did. I backed out of the driveway and told myself today was going to be a good day.

Another Night In

After several strenuous weeks into his freshman year of college and only just a few days into his eight-week probation sentence sanctioned on behalf of the university in response to committing the worst violation known to the administration—this, of course, referring to "the incident," a.k.a. being caught red-handed trying to smuggle a friend from a different university into his dorm room—we now observe the vices, temptations, and thoughts that circulate BJ's mind on any given particular night.

RIGHT BRAIN. What are you doing?

ME. Let's see. Well, besides playing the harmonica and making toilet wine, I think all of this "free time" on my hands is best spent reading.

RIGHT BRAIN. Oh, that's right, how could I forget? I'm sure there's nothing else a freshman boy could be doing at this hour. What with you being incarcerated and all, how else would you be able to appreciate the absolute and mysterious wonders of…of… what textbook is he reading again?

LEFT BRAIN. Latin. He's studying for his ancient Latin exam this Friday.

RIGHT BRAIN. Ah yes, Latin, the language of love. Didn't we just learn the other day how common it was for the Romans to wrestle completely nude and strip down publicly to defecate? How romantic.

LEFT BRAIN. All right, that's enough. Can you just let the poor boy study?

ME. Yes, thank you, left brain. How am I supposed to concentrate with you two going back and forth?

RIGHT BRAIN. Okay, okay. Point taken. I'll shut up…but did any of you notice the loud music coming from a few doors down? Sounds like they're having fun, but what do I know?

LEFT BRAIN. You just had to say it. I was trying to keep him distracted by helping him concentrate on this drawn-out Latin passage about…about…ah shit, I lost it.

ME. Guys, please, how am I supposed to focus when you two can't be quiet for more than ten seconds? Left brain, you know more than anyone I need to get a decent grade on this exam.

LEFT BRAIN. I mean yeah, but if we're using justified reasoning and logic here, shouldn't we take a little study break for like hmm… thirty minutes so we can come back fully focused instead of wasting time thinking about what's going on in that room a few doors down?

RIGHT BRAIN. Damn, maybe we're not so different after all, left brain. Just look at you wanting to take uncalculated chances.

LEFT BRAIN. This, coming from the one who's responsible for day-dreaming about that girl from Calabasas who sits next to us in our creative writing class. Did you forget you made him miss the entire lecture?

ME. Guys, you're both still missing the point. I'm not against having fun. Actually, reading this eleven-point font under this spotty desk lamp is killing me, but I have to get this done. Even if I wanted to go out, if I got caught by the RA, I'd be kicked off campus and then subjected to academic review by the university.

LEFT BRAIN. Granted, however, this is also the same university that serves you lukewarm synthetic meals out of a plastic bag you then have to take back to your room to eat alone.

RIGHT BRAIN. Yeah, that is pretty brutal, I have to say. I've still yet to be fully convinced your stomach has made a full recovery. How ya doing down there, buddy?

STOMACH. (…)

RIGHT BRAIN. He'll be fine, I'm sure.

LEFT BRAIN. And let's not forget the fact you've spent the last two weeks covering critical race theory in all of your courses, which consisted of lectures and presentations filled with jargon, ultimately boiling down to how much of an ignorant and shitty person you are because of your skin color.

ME. Oh, come on, it wasn't that bad.

RIGHT BRAIN. BJ, they drove your friend to call her parents with tears running down her face, questioning them if they had raised her to be racist.

ME. Okay, maybe it was that bad.

RIGHT BRAIN. So…what's stopping you from going to that party down the hall? I think that girl from Calabasas was totally feeling you. I heard she cheated on her boyfriend from back home with that one guy who looks like an Idaho potato. With that being said, I'm sure you could find a way to slide.

ME. Yeah…I'm gonna pass.

LEFT BRAIN. Why! You're at least a solid six.

ME. Wow, thanks, but I'm not really in the mood for that. You guys know I don't buy into the regularity of hookup culture. Someone always gets attached until they realize they don't actually matter to that person aside from when they are drunk or horny.

RIGHT BRAIN. No, I know what this is about. You're still not over Jennifer. I can feel it.

ME. What? That's not true, okay? Besides, she has a boyfriend now, and he's not too fond of our late-night FaceTime calls.

LEFT BRAIN. Psh, that guy? Acne? The one who you used to bully on the wrestling mat? The one who has control issues? I can't believe you're even wasting brainpower thinking about pizza face.

ME. Look, I was the one who ended things, remember? And I have no evidence to believe this guy is any worse for her than if we would've tried to make this thing work long distance. We're both too young, too free, to be tied down.

RIGHT BRAIN. Sure, but he's driving you out of her life completely, BJ! It's time to wake up. Call her.

ME. No.

LEFT BRAIN. Call her.

ME. No! I just can't, all right? Every time I call her, it feels like I'm ripping open a scar she'd be better off leaving be.

LEFT BRAIN. Doesn't she know you'd tell her everything if she'd just slide her thumb to the right?

ME. That's exactly why I can't. I have to let her move on even if she's the only person I can talk to.

RIGHT BRAIN. Well, shit, we've come this far, and you've already got your phone in your hand, so—and hear me out—how about we Snapchat some girls and see if they're awake?

ME. No. We can't keep doing this thing where we Snapchat the same girls who are just as lonely as I am and will do just about anything to get some attention.

LEFT BRAIN. That's right, BJ! We're all for women empowerment in case you didn't know, right brain.

ME. Oh, don't flatter yourself, left brain. You know I've just about had my fill of rampant destructive thoughts for the evening.

RIGHT BRAIN. Okay, we promise to be quiet, but that still doesn't solve the problem of your lack of compassion. How long before you realize the closest thing you've had to any level of human contact the past six weeks has been by virtue of your right hand? How much longer before you hesitate and stop yourself from scrolling through Jennifer's Instagram profile only to realize she's happier without you? How many more lonely nights are you willing to endure?

LEFT BRAIN. Hmm, impressive, right brain, perhaps even a bit inspiring. Maybe you were right about us being similar after all.

RIGHT BRAIN. Psh, it was nothing. If we're being honest, I'm still thinking about those naked Romans.

LEFT BRAIN. ...And you lost it. Now let's give the boy some rest. I think he's just starting to doze off.

RIGHT BRAIN. I'm with you on that one, left brain. Is it just me, or is he starting to bum you out more and more when he's awake? Anyways, I hope he realizes that he left his desk lamp on and he's drooling all over the textbook he needs for his 8:00 a.m. class.

Commencement

There are two definitions to the word *commencement*. The first: a new beginning or fresh start. The second: the ceremony in which diplomas are conferred on graduating students.

This story contains both.

Walking across the stage, I looked to my left. One hundred and twenty-six black caps and gowns stared back at me. My journey, my destiny, and my climb to the top was at its end. I grabbed a diploma cover to match my diploma that was already in a folder at home and smiled at the camera, broadcasting our ceremony to everyone at home. It wasn't great, but I knew it was better than what most other schools allowed. Although I had always thought these things were a bit anticlimactic. Realistically, there was no feasible way to capture the four years spent working toward that slip of paper or even a nod to the experiences outside of the classroom, which were, frankly, more important. Don't get me wrong, I was an A student with a GPA above a 4.0, but there was something about the afternoons spent on the football field, weekends out with friends, and shenanigans only a hormone-filled adolescent mind could think of that were priceless. The community that I now considered a part of me didn't know my name from the start, and it certainly wasn't going to wait for me to get adjusted. I was more or less thrown into the deep end from my first day off the plane, and I knew with that came one shot to go from the new kid to someone who would be remembered. By no stretch of the imagination was it going to be perfect, but then again, it was the only chance I had.

House Rules

I remember sitting in the passenger seat of my grandmother's Ford Escape on our way back from the Indianapolis Airport and awakening to the sound of her lecturing me on my new life. Her face was emotionless, and she had on dark-tinted sunglasses that resembled the ones the man with no eyes had from *Cool Hand Luke*. I already began to think I made a mistake.

"There are going to be rules around here, mister," she said, not taking her eyes off the road.

"I know, Grandma," I said in an attempt to get her to drop the subject.

"No, I mean it. You are fifteen years old, and I will not have you living with me if you don't abide by my rules," she said, with her facial expression unchanged.

"Grandma, I got it," I said, turning my back to her and trying to fall asleep once more.

"Well, all right then. Once we get you settled in, we'll swing by the school and get the documentation side of things squared away," she said, taking the Kokomo bypass exit. I drifted off as I questioned my decision not to say goodbye to any of my childhood friends. Most of them turned their backs on me or sought out new circles to join that didn't involve me, which was a lot to take in at fifteen. I was the one sitting at the end of the lunch table, I was the one on the sidelines, and I was the one excluded from group chats. Freshman year was one I never wanted to revisit.

I awoke to the sound of the garage door opening followed by my grandmother's voice urging me to get my duffel bag out of the trunk. That, paired with a suitcase full of sneakers, were the only two things I brought with me from Texas. After parking next to my late grandfather's prized convertible Mustang, she showed me to my room in the corner of the house. The house itself was comfortable but far from lavish. It was a one-story with a simple ranch-style concept and couldn't have been more than 1,700 square feet. The wood flooring and Lay-Z-Boy furnishings cascaded from one room into the next. It took me all of fifteen minutes to unpack my things once inside my room. The walls were bare, and the worn-down nightstand had two drawers full of extra bedsheets. *Why so many? Does she think I'm going to wet the bed? Another farcical gesture*, I thought. It wasn't until I shut the drawers that I noticed the Purdue comforter already on top of my bed.

"Your mom had me order it for you," she said, poking her head through the doorframe. She had always anticipated the day I'd announce my decision to attend Purdue, but that day never came. "The high school is gonna be closing soon. We'd better head over," she said, grabbing her purse in the other room. Shortly after that, I found myself in the guidance counselor's office discussing my class schedule. Posters of zebras and office knickknacks cluttered her desk. A sack of the freshman class's transcripts lay behind her.

"So you'll be a sophomore, right?" the counselor asked, clicking her mouse and gazing at her monitor.

"Yeah, and I already have my fine arts credit," I said, running my fingers through my hair.

"I can see that. Choir, was it?" she asked.

"Yeah," I said, lifting my ankle to rest on my knee while shaking my foot vigorously.

"All right, I think that does it. You want to see your class schedule?" she asked, turning her monitor around. I squinted my eyes to adjust them to her brightly lit LED screen.

1. Algebra II
2. Integrated Chemistry and Physics
3. &4 World Literature
5. Horticulture
6. Spanish II
7. Study Hall

"Looks great. Two small problems," I said, turning her screen back around.

"What's that?" she asked.

"I don't see the elective for football on there, and what's horticulture?" I asked.

"Oh well, horticulture is the class where you go inside the greenhouse every day and learn to grow crops. As for this football class, we don't offer that here," she said.

"So when am I supposed to lift weights or watch film?" I asked.

"Well, at practice, of course," she said, batting her eyes and shooting me a look that said enough questions. She continued by leaning in and saying, "Look, I get this is all so new to you, so the only advice I can offer you is this. What time does school start back up again in Texas?" she asked.

"Late August," I said. "Around the twenty-eighth."

"So why don't we think of this as an extended stay, hmm?" she said pristinely. "You're just checking out another school over the summer?" she said. "That's all."

"I guess," I said, planting both of my feet on the carpeted floor.

"Speaking of football, practice starts tomorrow. I better let you go so you can get some rest," she said, walking me out of her office.

I wrote down my thoughts on a PenPad I found tucked under the sheets in my drawer when I got back home. This was my only way of making sense of everything unfolding around me. After comparing the fifth Drake quote from "Too Much" to my current circumstances, I was beat. I had no idea where they were going to play me tomorrow or what was the caliber of the players I was going to be competing for a spot against. I was brainwashed by the cult or, how the parents see it, the religion that is high school football in Texas, and the only thing I was concerned with was securing a position on any team offense or defense. I hadn't played a competitive sport since the eighth grade due to a season-ending injury in a scrimmage during my freshman year, so naturally, my only concern was redemption.

Run It Back

The next day that would prove to be life-changing had arrived. Coach Hooker, head coach of the Rochester Zebras Football Team, had been hired just a few days prior to my arrival. While he had coached other sports and been a prominent figure in years past, he had taken a well-deserved stint away from the school cooperation and was now also in the business of looking to prove something. The varsity team posted a historically rough performance the year before, with a daunting record of 0–10. Besides having the worst record in school history, the previous coach was also under fire for various accusations, including butting heads with influential community figures. He was practically run out of town and resigned in a matter of days.

Our first team meeting was inside of the weight room, and the players that he had previously coached swarmed him like flies. I for one did not join the frenzy. On top of not knowing the guy at all, the weight room was small and stuffy. From what looked to be the remains of a classroom with no windows and inadequate ventilation, I began to question how every team in the school used it. The weights were lined with rust, and the water fountain inside didn't even work. It was a step down compared to the 6A three-million-dollar facility I was used to, but on the other hand, that was a big reason why I moved in the first place. Texas-sized egos plagued everyone involved in the school cooperation, causing them to be more obsessed with appearance than anything else. I was able to put two and two together when I stumbled upon swastikas carved into the toilet seats, but rather than address this, the new bill that was passed funded the expansion of the stadium that already seated twelve thousand attendees. There is a price that comes with having the most uniform combinations in the state and a jumbotron on both the inside and outside of a megaplex.

After the crowd died down, Coach Hooker passed out a lifting workout he had typed while giving instructions.

"I want deep squats. None of that half-ass effort you guys call technique," coach said, dressed in his khaki cargo shorts and tucked-in vintage Rochester Football T-shirt. "And don't even think about giving me the tired spiel about how you want to preserve the longevity of your knees. I only got you for four years max," he said with a black plastic whistle dangling on his lower lip. The fifty-seven-year-old was the embodiment of old school. During our first lift as a team, he sat on the wooden table propped up against the entrance and preached of our new offensive game strategy. We were going to run the Wing-T offense. A simple concept, if done correctly, with the sole purpose of running the ball down the opposing team's throat. Of course, this was another key difference when it came to Hooker's vision. He preferred hard-nosed football and a battle at the line of scrimmage every play compared to the flashy air raid style of play that was claiming the larger schools around the country.

Once we finished our last set, he called for us to take a knee around the table to discuss our practice plan and get a breakdown. "We will have practice most weekdays, with some of those being two-a-days. Once the season begins and school starts, we will have practice Monday through Thursday and, of course, games on Friday. Saturday mornings, we will meet back here for film, a light lift, and a cooldown stretch. Any questions?" he asked. Crickets chirped in the background as we blankly stared up at him. "Lastly, our team motto for this year is to avoid being a jabroni. Did any of you watch The Rock growing up?" He asked. "Can anyone tell me what a jabroni is?" One of the players spoke up from the back.

"A jabroni is a fool, sir."

"That's right, an embarrassment and someone who is notorious for making mental mistakes. We can't have those. They'll cost us games," he said as the brim of his hat covered his eyes and a smirk appeared. "Now let's get a breakdown. Zebras on three. One, two, three, Zebras!" we all shouted in unison. I took a moment to rack some of the dumbbells that were left out and must have caught the eye of Coach because when he spoke, it caught me off guard.

"Hey, you're the Texan, aren't you?" he asked, leaning on the side of the rack.

"Uh, yessir, I am," I said, bending over to grab another.

"Have you ever played quarterback before?" he asked.

"No, sir, mostly corner," I answered.

"Surely, with those cannons, you've got to be kidding," he said, chuckling and squeezing my pale, skinny bicep. I chuckled, too, and asked why. "The JV team is looking for a quarterback, and I think you might be the guy," he said.

"Are you sure, Coach?" I asked, puzzled. "I mean, there's gotta be someone else more qualified than me."

"You'd be surprised. This freshman class is full of scrubs, and around here, we don't exactly make cuts," he said.

"I mean, I'll give it a shot, but I've never done anything like that," I said.

"You'll be fine. Our playbook is mostly run plays as it is. I'll make sure to get it to you by the end of the week," he said over his shoulder while walking out of the weight room. The upperclassmen drove away and did doughnuts in the parking lot while the freshmen and sophomores who didn't yet have their license waited for their parents to pick them up outside of the school.

"So you're new, huh?" one of the players asked. He was a small boy with a blond buzz cut and buckteeth who stood up to my shoulder. I myself couldn't have been more than five feet nine at the time.

"Yeah," I said briefly, looking him off.

"Well, I'm a freshman too," he said, still gazing up at me.

"No, no, I'm not a freshman. I am a sophomore. I'm just new to Rochester, to Indiana for that matter," I said, pulling my practice bag over my shoulder.

"Ohhh okay. I'm Jon, by the way, Jon Kelly. What's your name?" he asked.

"My name is BJ Barnes," I said, now looking down at him.

He laughed and said, "Really, you're not messing with me?"

"No," I said, now slightly annoyed.

"Well, with a name like that, your parents must hate you," he said.

"No, actually, they don't even live here," I replied.

"Oh, so they just don't want you," he said.

"No. They didn't beat me, they didn't touch me, and yes, they could provide for me. We did fairly well for that matter," I said, as my face turned red. "I only moved because I despised my old school. Down there, I was just a number, and it hit me that I needed a change of scenery when my teacher didn't know my name as I went to turn in my final."

"Okay, okay, I was just asking," he said, taking a step back. "I had a rough year, too, ya know. I got hit by a car that tried to keep going," he said, taking a seat on the grass.

"Oh my gosh, I'm so sorry. If it helps, I couldn't tell," I said, uneasy of where the conversation had gone.

"No, it's fine. I'm all good now. It's just when that happened, for the first time in my life, I felt completely helpless. These middle school and high school bullies may think they're tough, but deep down, they're just pussies. Scared pussies," he said, with a laugh that exposed his buckteeth once more. He was the Tasmanian Devil with a foul mouth and a Napoleon complex, but he had a point. I always admired how he was never afraid of a fight. He and whomever he faced knew beating him senseless was a waste of time, so most of the time, he would get away with lipping off. My grandma pulled up to the curb not long after to take me home, and I hopped inside.

"Looks like someone made a friend," she said, turning to look at me, leaving one hand on the wheel.

"If that's what you want to call it," I said, fastening my seat belt.

"You know, you'd make more if you smiled," she said.

"I know, I know. Let me be," I said as we passed the Kroger gas station.

"Fine," she said. "But you're going to tell me how practice went."

"I'm the quarterback. Well, the JV quarterback anyway."

"Well, that's just great. I'll have to tell Karmin and the coffee gals," she said, hitting the garage door button attached to the sun visor. Karmin was the leader of this so-called coffee group. She met with these coffee gals at various coffee shops around town on the weekdays, and believe it or not, they were a powerful force when it came to authority in Rochester. Some of them served as city council members, and others had connections to influential figures that ran as deep and as far as you'd like to look. The funny thing was, they wouldn't let just anyone in either. They were a selective group, and when a new grandma wanted to join, the process was similar to a job application. I dubbed them the Grandma Mafia, and it stuck. From then on out, there wasn't a girl I talked to or friend I invited over without them running a background check or knowing about beforehand. The last four weeks of summer meshed together with my grandma pulling me out of bed at 7:00 a.m. to go to coffee and the afternoons dedicated to Coach Hooker teaching me how to run a huddle. It was time for the first-day-of-school nightmare that was having seating charts, finding your classes, and being unsure of where to sit at lunch.

My grandma drove me up to the front of the school and told me to smile before saying goodbye. I walked through the front door, and right off the bat, the front office was flooded with unhappy students wanting a schedule change. Once I made it past the mob, I figured out where most kids congregated before the start of first period. Our school mascot, Zebbie the Zebra, was a life-size stuffed animal that stood upright inside of a plastic cage. It was right outside of the cafeteria and had seating all around. The cage was a new addition in response to the kidnapping of Zebbie in a foiled senior prank the year before. I didn't know anyone besides Jon and a few other JV players, so I made conversation with a few other frightened freshmen until the first period bell rang. It wasn't until practice later that day when I figured out Jon was late to school because the meth lab across the street from his house blew up, and it was protocol for the buses not to breach a tenth of a mile radius when en route. After digging up soil in fifth period and mumbling my way to a first letter grade of a D– in Spanish, it was time for practice.

Our first game was against the Logansport Berries that week. Yes, the Zebras versus the Berries. I'm not sure why the correlation between oddball mascots and Northern Indiana ever existed, but this was just one of the many quirks I came to discover in my three years there. It was just one of ten games I would play as the team's quarterback, and while it was far from anything the varsity team was accomplishing, we finished with a .500 record. Head JV coach and varsity receiver coach, Coach Beck, mentioned it was better than the year before, and to a team where winning was becoming more of a relic, I was glad I could at least get some wins under our belts. Beck took me under his wing and offered guidance to me when Hooker was too busy with varsity. When he told me he made it to the North/South All-State game, I knew I had to do the same. Meanwhile, Coach Hooker led the varsity team to an impressive 7–3 that was cut short due to a missed extra point in the first round of playoffs. The Zebras were back, and so was my charisma. I wasn't satisfied, though, and wouldn't be for quite some time.

Tunnel Vision

There was a missing piece. Not all the Texas high school traditions were disreputable. Walking out of RHS and onto the football field didn't exactly set the tone of the game. We needed a tunnel. Even the little league teams in the Houston area had tunnels, yet in all the twenty games I either played in or watched from the varsity sideline, not one of them ran out of a tunnel. As a sophomore who had little to show for himself thus far, I thought if I could bring a new tradition to the school I was just learning how to be a part of, I would surely be remembered for my efforts.

During study hall that afternoon, I emailed the athletic director and informed him of my idea. I had found a tunnel that was not only affordable but was in the shape of a zebra head. He had never heard of such a thing and was on board so long as I found a sponsor to fund the project. I contacted the local sports supply store, The Winning Edge, with my pitch, and the owner agreed to have it processed but mentioned I'd still have to find an investor. Within a couple of weeks, a sponsor reached out to the athletic director and offered to fund the entire idea. He was the owner of a local insurance agency that had been passed down from his father, who actually started the company. Normally, this detail might not have carried any significance, but it would go on to speak volumes as the process of retaining a tunnel for the team continued. I knew I'd be on varsity next year, and to have the tunnel attached to my legacy would be quite the feat for a fifteen-year-old newcomer. After Saturday morning practice, I went to thank him personally. I walked into his tiny building, saw him behind the front counter, and introduced myself.

"Well, it's nice to meet you, BJ," he said, resting his forearms on the countertop. "What can I do for you?" he asked.

"Well, I'm actually one of the players on the football team, and I just wanted to drop by and thank you personally for purchasing the inflatable tunnel," I said, reaching out my arm. Before I could mention the excitement the athletic director and I felt, he shook my hand and responded arrogantly.

"It was no problem, really. I have always wanted to get this done. My wife and I have been in talks with the athletic director for years, and this year presented an opportunity we just couldn't turn down," he said as I retracted my arm. "Yep, when the Mrs. and I found this tunnel, we both agreed we had to buy it for the team." I was bewildered. By not knowing who I was, he made the mistake of passing me off as one of the dozens of townsfolk who blindly idolized him, but I could never figure out why. He was handed the business on a silver platter, along with all its clientele and capital. He had amounted to nothing and was rewarded with a billboard of him and his family standing next to the tunnel outside of the local Arby's. He noticed my facial expression and followed up with a question. "Hey, how'd you even know about the tunnel? The athletic director and I have kept this thing on a closed circuit."

Instead of calling him out in his own establishment and in front of the two contractors behind me, I responded by saying, "Oh, I just overheard the athletic director on the phone in his office and figured I'd beat the crowd. This kind of thing is bound to get some attention."

"Well, that's what we're hoping for," he said, smiling. "Anything else I can do ya for? You wouldn't be interested in a quote, would you?" he said, chuckling and nudging one of his employees.

"Nah, I think I'm all right," I said, stone-faced. I didn't even bid farewell before I turned around and shut the glass door behind me. I was at a loss for words. Why would a respected businessman steal the credit from a fifteen-year-old kid who was new to the community just looking to do it some good? To this day, I still do not know the answer, and it didn't help that his wife contacted me a few days later telling me to drop it. That was one of the first lessons I'd learn the hard way, and after that, it didn't take me long to realize what people would do for power in a small town. After knowing it was out of my hands, I let it go and was on to finding the next thing that would cement my legacy. This soon became an obsession. Every morning, I'd wake up with the same mentality of thirsting for an opportunity to prove myself, and that opportunity would come but not before a devastating blow.

The Unthinkable

Junior year had arrived. One down, two to go. The summer before upheld every promise of warm and wet bodies, but alas, it was time to say sayonara to my first lakeshore summer. This was not an empty exchange, however, because with the end of summer marked the beginning of fall, and with fall came football. Suiting up for a practice with full pads was never fun but especially not in the middle of an August heatwave. With the disappointing loss still circulating throughout Hooker's mind, he installed a new warm-up routine that consisted of running thirty yards after every stretch. He, as well as almost any other coach I had played for, swore at the roots to every loss was being ill-prepared and unconditioned. A quarter of the way through warm-ups, the entire team was sweating through their gear and panting like dogs. In the moment, I thought Hooker was so amused he needed a minute to recollect himself behind the equipment shed. He was never against having fun. He'd even created trivia questions on the practice plan and offered prizes to the first person who knew the answer. Strangely enough, it would usually be me, with the seniors distracted by snorting preworkout and bickering over what song to play.

The first few weeks of the season followed in this succession, except Hooker's trips behind the equipment shed were becoming more frequent and sometimes came without warning. Rumors started to fabricate as to why he would go behind the shed, but I chose to turn the other way. Late in the season, we got our answer. It was week 9, and we had our toughest matchup of the season against the Maconaquah Braves. We got word as soon as we boarded the buses that Coach Hooker would not be coaching us for this game due to unspecified reasons. Whether it was the mixture of sleet and snow that coated the field throughout the duration of the game or the fact Hooker wasn't on our sideline, our heads just weren't in it that night. We lost, 28–8, and had several injuries.

The next morning before the start of film, the defensive coordinator, Coach Hughes, informed us of Hooker's situation. We all sat on the black benches in the varsity bay and idly listened.

"So as you all are well aware, Coach Hooker has had some health issues these past few months. What you nor any of us knew is what exactly was going on. Last night, Coach wanted to be at the game more than anything, but what I'm about to tell you made that virtually impossible. In Fort Wayne, the doctors found a tumor inside of his brain. As for the size of it, we were hoping it would be small. Around four centimeters. It was not. It was four inches, roughly the size of a notecard."

We all sat there in shock and disbelief. *Why him? Why now? Can he be cured?* Hughes had had a run-in with cancer himself and lost a leg in the process, confining him to a mobility chair a few years prior.

"It is thought to be stage four. As for treatment options, his return to school or coaching, I have no idea. The only thing I ask of you all is to pray." Playoffs were next week, and we had just been handed our own asses on and off the field. As much as I hated the thought of it, the rumors had been true. Coach Hooker had been going behind the shed to vomit, all the while never letting anyone know. Never once did he ask for our sympathy or our pity. Instead, he fought until he couldn't anymore, and all he asked of us now was to do the same.

We ended up breaking the playoff drought by winning our first game, 55–7. The next game wouldn't be so simple, as we faced the defending state champs. While we tried our best to pull off a late fourth-quarter comeback, the four fumbles in the first half were too much to overcome. I knew this feeling all too well. It was the same feeling that brought me back down to earth when we lost to our rivals who snapped our undefeated season in week 7. It was the same feeling when the senior class graduates leaving the classes beneath them to step up. It was the same feeling that came when fall gave way to winter. When the leaves shriveled up and the branches ran dry; when all outside activities ceased and gave way to the polar vortex, and this time, it was inescapable.

The fearsome front of senior defensive linemen who had been unstoppable all season wept like kids. Besides, it being the last game any of them would play, we all felt the unrest that came with fearing for Hooker's life. Sadly, that unrest wouldn't last much longer. After an arduous struggle, Coach Hooker passed away on January 3, 2019, at the age of fifty-nine. His viewing was held that Sunday at the school. When I arrived with Jon, the school parking lot was full, and the zebra tunnel had been blown up outside of the entrance in his honor. It was an inspiration to see the entire town supporting his legacy, minus the sleazy insurance owner who stood by the tunnel, waving to people walking by as if this event was to honor him. Jon and I scoffed at the very sight of him as we made our way into the gymnasium and couldn't believe the line of people paying their respects. We stood in that gym for an hour and a half listening to Chicago's "Saturday in the Park" and Elton John's "Bennie and the Jets" on repeat as the line that snaked from each baseline shortened one by one. It was almost therapeutic to hear the stories people were sharing with one another as we all waited in line. Some had photos, while others wore their letterman jackets dating back decades. That afternoon, we were all teenagers. That afternoon, we left behind the intrusions of phone calls, emails, and punch cards, and embraced life for what it really is.

He was put to rest the following Monday in a Lutheran Church in the nearby town of Logansport, Indiana. I was one of maybe a dozen students who bothered attending the service. While it was a somber experience through and through, it was hysterical to see the jocks who were a part of the biyearly church crowd struggle to find verses as they frantically flipped through the Bible. School never was the same after he passed. In fact, I don't think the community ever entirely recovered. Touching Hooker's legacy was never an option, but evoking the same energy and pride he did that afternoon in the gymnasium was my only goal for the next year and a half. Time was waning, and my only mission was to unify the same city that made me. The city that housed crack fiends, freeloaders, and girls who were too young to be mothers was the same city that had lakefront mansions, farming dynasties, and an educational system that provided every student with a MacBook. I didn't have much authority, albeit, but if scoring a touchdown, ringing the Salvation Army bell, or broadcasting informative content about the school's nicotine crisis carried any weight, I was going to see it through.

Montage

As tacky as it might be, Rocky was a huge influential figure for me in my time in Rochester, and as with any *Rocky* movie, I needed a montage if I was going to climb the notorious high school hierarchy. I first needed a coach, a father figure, really. I had moved away from my loving parents in Texas for too many reasons to register, most of which pertained to school rather than them; however, they also had their fair share of troubles.

My father was rarely around growing up due to a rather messy divorce that occurred when I was in kindergarten. My mother won custody, which meant the designated time I was allowed to spend with him was every other weekend. I first got wind of this when I was picked up from daycare. At the time, I didn't know what to make of it, just sitting in the back of my mother's silver minivan. Her wild green eyes looked at me through the rearview mirror as I sat propped up by the booster seat. Residue sprinkles and icing stained the sides of my mouth blue. They were the remains from a classmate's sixth birthday party, and the red Fruit of the Loom shirt I was wearing was sticking up on one end of my collar. There were many fights drawn tracing back to my sloppy eating habits or appearance. I was a kid, for God's sake, but my sister and I couldn't help feel astray all the same. When I did see my father, almost every stay at his house would consist of playing catch in the field at the end of the cul-de-sac and curling up in a beanbag on the carpeted floor, while falling asleep to the sound of an old monster movie. By the time I grew out of this, he had moved out of the suburbs and into an apartment downtown. He did this for two reasons: one, to be closer to his new girlfriend, and two, because the two-hour commute each way had deteriorated anything close to a soul he had left. I saw him even less then. He worked hard, but I knew even then I never wanted an office job. The worn-down trend on his tires spoke for themselves.

Back home with my mom, things couldn't be more different. While she herself loved me more than just about anything, she made the decision to work more and be at home less. Not that she didn't enjoy my sister and my company, but she felt we'd have a better childhood if she could provide everything a two-parent household could. This meant Disney cruises and trips to Europe but less time at home. She'd go on to ultimately regret this decision in the long run. I don't know if it would have made that much of a difference. We still made time for each other, and my sister and I had anything a kid growing up could desire. We moved into a gated community right across the street from the high school, and come to think of it, I'm almost certain she was the only single mother there. On her salary alone, I was able to keep up with the middle school rat race of wearing the best clothes and rocking the best sneakers. It was nice to "straight stunt on them hoes," as some of my public school classmates would call it, but there were many vivid mornings when I'd get up from school to see my mother already gone. This would last five years until, of course, I finished my freshman year. With almost a thousand kids per class, there was still no one to look up to. Now wrapping up my junior year, I was looking in a mirror. I had come far, but I wasn't finished.

Arguably the most talented senior class the football team had seen in years had just graduated. Except most of them didn't even leave the greater area. I didn't want to believe it, but just as the class before them and most classes before that class, the seniors who had dominated defenses and obliterated offenses didn't even bother pursuing a college career or a degree. Instead, they spun the lie that was as old as time and used the excuse that was so commonly known in the Midwest as "joining the workforce." I had always known of the Midwestern grit and grind. That came with the territory. Hoosiers were scrappy, but this was not the case with our seniors. After graduation, the same guys I looked up to were still going to the same parties, with the same goal of "bagging a high school chick." They weren't contributing to society, and they sure as shit weren't attending trade school. It never irritated me that they didn't seek post-second-ary education. It irritated me that they squandered any opportunities they had to share their gifts. My heroes fell void to clinging to the golden days, and while they might have literally been blocks away, they wouldn't be on the field with me next fall. Some part of me was grateful for that. Without a definitive end, I might have followed in their footsteps.

Regardless of their close proximity, it was time for the junior class to fill in the role of the next man up. Seeing as how we needed all the help we could get, Edward's father, Brad, stepped forward and offered to train Edward, Bruce, and me. He was a state trooper, and while he wasn't perfect, he was the father figure I needed. I might have been on varsity, but my stats were nothing close to the All-State potential I knew I had. Two targets and one catch for nine yards was all I had to show through eleven games my junior year. Despite this unimpressive stat line, I would go on to dwarf tenfold in the first game of my senior season, I was a part of every drive, but due to the team's heavy reliance on the run and lack of targets, I could not fill the shoes I saw fit.

This is where Brad stepped in. He used the summer mornings before work to conduct whatever hellish workouts he could conceive. From borderline waterboarding us on the end of his pier when the water was still frozen over from the night before to encouraging us to hold a maul over our heads for forty-five minutes straight, Brad was determined to turn us into men. He did this all from the comfort of his own lawn chair while referencing any *Top Gun*, *A Few Good Men*, *Karate Kid*, and yes, *Rocky* quotes that came to mind. He would have done it out of purely good intentions, but I think he also longed to coach once more.

After chasing us in his police cruiser and blaring Queen while we jogged through the morning mist, he would always invite us inside for a breakfast buffet where he would extend his daily wisdom. Edward would practically plug his ears and roll his eyes to the back of his skull as Brad preached. It was a virtual certainty Brad would end his message by saying, "Always wear sunscreen," a reference to the Baz Luhrmann song I wouldn't figure out until much later when

I was away at school. In short, Brad had a way of bringing out the best in all of us. He wouldn't take the credit for it, but he was the force behind a majority of my achievements, and the only favor he asked in return was that we pass it on. By that he meant when we found ourselves reaching his age, all he asked was that we offer food, shelter, and wisdom to those younger and in dire need of it. He took that same boy with sprinkles around his mouth that now had acne peppered across his chin and transformed him into an athlete with unparalleled ambition.

Nostalgia

Now taking my seat at graduation, I watched as the rest of the student body passed me by as they grabbed their corresponding diploma covers. It was over. Graduating was an experience I could only compare to walking out of a dark movie theater after seeing a popular summer blockbuster. Everyone was familiar with the experience, yet when it was all said and done, I couldn't help to feel inspired while struggling to adjust all the same. It never mattered how much someone's family made. It never mattered what clique someone belonged to. It never mattered how smart someone was or how they dressed. Rochester Community High accepted and embraced one another time and time again. I had never had a permanent home, but for those three years, I was one with a whole. I discovered a community that relied and leaned on each other. People who supported local businesses and loved thy neighbor. Individuals more concerned with attending church than country club. Values and goals were shared by the community as opposed to just being advertised on billboards and jumbotrons to make hopeful mayors seem more appealing.

Somewhere hidden among the corn husks and silos was a town right off the Indiana interstate. The five-thousand people who called it home might be easily overlooked, but if there was one guarantee that reigned true, it was that there would be no replacing the support Rochester lent its own. Eventually, a boy would stumble at its doorstep seeking refuge. Only hoping for a seat at the table, this boy would be given a chance to sit with its finest. He'd first learn to fall; he'd then learn how to fly. He'd be given every tool imaginable to help him succeed, and in the blink of an eye, his venture would expire before he even had time to react. He now fantasized of a time in the distant future with uncertainty. There, all his high school peers were just a few doors down. He waved as he picked up the morning newspaper, and the sprinklers watered his sun-scorched lawn. His kids gazed through the doorway and held on tight to his leg, attempting to make sense of the world we all dove headfirst into.

Journal 5

A Deer in Headlights

The leaves on the tree outside of my friend's dorm room window were a translucent red that gave way to the incoming moonlight. The air was crisp and cold as a slight breeze snuck in through the screen. "Can you close your window?" I asked. "It's freezing in here."

"No, leave it open. I'll tell you when I want it closed." He jarred back. Bruce was very particular about the temperature in his room. As a matter of fact, he was particular about most things when it came to his room. The room was in shambles 95 percent of the time, except when he was expecting a girl over, which was a rarity in itself. Solo cups and beer cans claimed the top of his dresser at the foot of his bed. Nail clippings and dirty clothes soaked with sweat were scattered across the floor. His sheets that were never washed once were always bundled up in a ball in the top-left corner of his bed. The trash can next to his desk was overflowing with ghosts of meal's past. But boy, if someone forgot their cup or left a coat behind, they would never hear the end of it. The other bed across the room was the only place to sit in his double-sized dorm and was the spot for Friday nights during COVID-19. Since Wherewithal didn't allow more than a few people in a dorm at a time, most nights, our gatherings would be limited to Bruce, Ray, and me. Ray didn't count as a girl in Bruce's eyes because she was just one of us. One of the boys.

Ray was the odd man out when it came to us meeting up because while we weren't disobeying the occupancy rule, she was stationed to another residence hall, which meant coming over to Cam Hulltoe Hall was against the rules. She was always a trooper when it came to coming over, knowing that she could be written up; she still did it anyway. I was already on probation for inviting a friend from another school on campus grounds, and Bruce was never one to leave his surroundings.

"Ew! Bruce, it smells like mildew and dirty laundry in here," Ray said while opening the door.

"Then leave. Nobody asked you to come here, Ray," Bruce said with visible frustration.

"Actually, you did about five minutes ago," Ray said, shutting the door behind her with a YETI Rambler in her left hand.

"Woah, woah, woah, we came here to have fun and unwind. It's been a long week, and we need to relax. Now, what movie do you guys want to watch on Netflix?" I said, leaning up in the other bed. They both shrugged with disinterest. It never really mattered what movie was on because we'd end up talking through most of it about gossip and current events anyway. We were all lonely as hell, and if it weren't for each other's company, we never would have watched half of these movies on our own time. On this specific September night, *Secret Life of Pets 2* was the movie of choice. After another loaded exchange, Ray managed to squabble one of the three available blankets away from Bruce. According to him, he needed all three. She and I sat next to each other on the twin bed, sharing the yellow-and-green hand-tied Oregon blanket. Bruce always swore jokingly he would play football there, but deep down, he knew this aspiration would always be out of reach. Bruce lay down in his bed with his ankle-high, white, Nike socks halfway off, cusping the sole of his feet.

"What? It helps me stay cool," he said time and time again. After the movie had run its course, Bruce was on the verge of falling asleep. In a sleep-induced state of dreariness, he was able to mutter, "Can you guys get out of my room now?"

"Sure," I replied. Ray sat up and thanked Bruce for his hospitality while I folded the blanket. Ray and I circumnavigated our way through the mounds of paraphernalia in his room and found the door. "See ya tomorrow, bud." I let out with a sigh, shaking my head.

"Okay," he said with his head stuffed in his pillow stained with yellow spots. "And make sure you close my door."

"Will do," Ray and I said synchronously. The door clicked shut as Ray stood behind me.

"I don't want to go back yet," Ray said with eyes resembling a lost puppy.

"It's eleven thirty," I said with a puzzled expression.

"I know, but it's also a Friday night. Have a sense of adventure," she replied.

"All right, we can go to my dorm, but you know how tight it is," I said, walking down the hall. The giddy footsteps that followed spoke for her. We arrived at my door, and I pulled out my key as she watched over my shoulder. "Here it is," I said with a chuckle.

"Oh my God, you really do have Harry Potter's closet for a room," she said, with her mouth wide open.

"Apparently, this is what $66,000 a year gets you," I said sarcastically. "So what do you want to do? Do you have anything in mind?" I asked.

"Oh, I don't know. I guess I was hoping we could just talk to one another," she said, setting her YETI cup down on my desk. What was once a twenty-ounce container full of clear liquor was now reduced to droplets at the bottom of her glass. She noticed me staring at the cup for a considerable amount of time, to which she said, "Shhh, I'm fine. I just want to talk."

To be completely honest, I was exhausted, but I was just getting to know her, and we were seamlessly getting closer to each other. I didn't want to let her down or ruin the mood, so I invited her to sit atop my bed. My bed was the only place we could both sit comfortably, and even that was hard enough with the ceiling caving in right above it. We somehow managed to squeeze side by side on the mattress with our legs dangling off the side and our backs propped up against the wall. Sounds of *The Office* playing through the paper-thin walls could be overheard from Jacob, the guy next door, but that didn't stop us.

"So why Wherewithal? Why did you choose to come here?" she asked.

"Oh, I don't know, the same reasons as everyone else, I suppose." Which was a pathetic excuse to a thoughtful question. I didn't enjoy opening up to other people, never have. She saw straight through it.

"No, c'mon, BJ. I'm serious. Why did you choose to come here?" she asked while her eyes darted back and forth at mine as if she was deciding which one to look at.

"Well, for starters, I was given a chance to play football again, which is a huge part of me coming here, but on top of that, when I visited, I felt as if my future was here. I know that sounds corny, but with Media Fellows and the close proximity to home, it just seemed like this is where I needed to be," I said.

"Now those are reasons. I don't know why you can't just be real with me. Do you just not trust me or what?" she questioned.

"It's not that," I said, staring blankly at the wall in front of me. "I am just very careful of who I let in."

"What? Don't tell me you have some broken heart sob story. Did someone take advantage of you?" she asked, poking my rib cage and giggling.

"That's exactly it, if you want to know the truth," I said, laughing and refocusing on her.

"All right, enough about me. I want to know about you. Why are you so nice to Bruce when literally everyone else, especially women, won't even speak to him?" I asked.

"Because I can read him. I know Bruce through and through even though I've only known him for two weeks," she said without hesitation.

"No, no, no, you can't call me out for having half-ass answers and then do the same," I said with a grin. "Tell me how you can read him and how you think you know him so well."

"Well, I can tell he comes from a somewhat rough household. I know he has trouble letting people see the real him, even more so than you. And finally, I know he's afraid of judgment more than anything else despite putting on the tough-guy act," she said, crossing her legs.

"You're good. I'll give you that," I said, nodding, with a skeptical look on my face.

"Duh, I wanna be a psychologist. That's my major," she said, flaunting.

"Do me then, if you're so gifted," I said.

"Nah, you're not worth the time," she said playfully.

"Ouch, you really got me there," I said, teasing her right back. A few hours went by like this until the conversation died off once and for all. "Jeez, it's two thirty. I had no idea," I said. We better get you back to your dorm.

"Just hang on a minute, party pooper. Let's listen to a song or two before I leave," she said enthusiastically.

"I don't know, Ray. It's pretty late," I said with caution. Before I even finished that thought, she hooked up to my speaker and started blaring music at full volume. This time with my voice raised, I begged her to turn down the music. It was no use. It was completely drained out by the sound of Travis Scott. It could be worse. She had good taste. I thought about Jacob next door and felt awful. He must have been sound asleep, only to be awoken by the lyrics of "It's Lit." After a few tracks, I was able to get her calmed down enough to disconnect from my speaker. "Hey, it's almost 3:00 a.m. Don't you think it's time to call it a night yet?" I proposed. She wasn't wasted, but she wasn't sober either.

"Yeah, I am pretty tired," she said, lowering her hands from above her head. "Would you mind if I spent the night?" she asked, with her eyes wide. The lost-puppy act had returned. This concept was always so taboo to me. The very thought of her spending the night scared me to death. I had been against the idea of a girl sleeping over initially, but after heavy persuasion, my arm was twisted. *It's not like we'll do anything,* I told myself. *It's just two people sleeping next to each other.*

"Eh, why not," I said, trying to be as suave as possible. She squealed with excitement and took off her coat. I turned around to untie my shoes and placed them off to the side. Sure enough, when I turned back around, she had taken off her clothes, leaving only a very revealing bra and thong strapped onto her showcase body.

"You don't mind, do you?" she said in a disoriented yet inviting tone. "It's just so hot in here."

"Uhh, no, not at all," I replied. This would be my downfall. I had always had a problem with telling people what I really thought. She wasn't wrong, though. It was pretty hot in my dorm. I regretfully mirrored her actions and did the same, removing my shirt and shorts. Somehow, I thought it'd be less awkward this way. The only thing preserving my dignity was a pair of *Space Jam* boxer briefs. After what seemed like an eternity of awkwardness, we got into bed. She tucked herself under the sheets while I remained on top of the comforter. One part of me insisted I keep this charade going, but finally, the other half prevailed. I knew this wasn't the right time. On account of us just getting to know one another and the notable amount of alcohol she had consumed, I didn't want to force anything either of us would regret.

"Aren't you gonna get underneath the covers?" she said, confused.

"Nah, I think I'll just stay up here for a while," I said as my eyes nervously surveyed the room, avoiding eye contact at all costs.

"Okay," she said while turning over. I was mortified, to say the least. Any other guy on campus would have jumped at the opportunity. I did the opposite and felt like a helpless kid all the same. I tossed and turned all night. There wasn't a moment I got more than fifteen minutes of sleep at a time.

I was already awake when her iPhone alarm dinged to signal the start of a new day. "Hey, how'd you sleep?" she asked, fixing her hair.

My hair was sticking up when I responded with a very unconvincing "Great."

"I slept so well," she said, stretching her arms as she got out of bed. "Hey, you don't mind if I borrow a shirt, do you?" she questioned.

"Here, let me find you one," I said, reaching for the closet. "Will this one work?" I asked, holding up a blue cotton long sleeve with my hometown lake on it.

"That's perfect," she replied. She put the shirt on and the black jeans from the night before as I grabbed her shoes.

"Here ya go."

"Aw, thank you," she said through a yawn. I showed her to the door, a distance of about four feet, and opened it quietly.

"Hope you had fun," I said.

"Of course, I did. Thanks for having me," she whispered, going in for a side hug. She slowly closed the door behind her, and all traces of the light coming in from the hallway were snuffed out.

Stay the Course

It's been a quiet few months, that I can't hide
To think I haven't seen your face since last September when we both
sat on your porch swing and cried

In the last year, I've tried to start a new life separate from yours
And I see that you've found a new man to help even the scores

But this was never a message disguised as a Trojan horse
To pretend that my life has turned out so much better than yours

No, this message is rather direct and applies to just about everyone
that comes to mind
As sad as it is, I'm afraid in these trying times we've all left something
behind

Sure, the list goes on and on, but let's be honest, none of us are the
same people as we were when this whole thing started
How could you not help feeling like your life has completely departed?

At school, the sex shops are open and the churches are closed
I mean, c'mon, the girls are unclothed and fully disposed

Professors try diligently to indoctrinate the vulnerable freshmen
in a large-scale attempt to meet the criteria of the agenda they've all
invested in

Kids drown themselves in alcohol in a room by themselves to cope
with the inescapable fact that they're all alone

Of course, this is still deemed "safe" so long as they're six feet apart
and stay on top of their student loans

But before you and your friends allow yourselves to be consumed by
remorse,
I have some advice: stay the course

Back home it appears a new era is upon us
Houses that were home to friends' families are now listed for sale as
parents downsize and adjust

The same friendships everyone swore would last forever have just
started to sever
While those who never left town lie to anyone they come across, trying desperately to pass off their lives have never been better

Peers from the past pretend they are too busy or so far removed from
their days in high school they'd rather not waste their time speaking
to someone from their community
Note, these will be the same ones that randomly email you fifteen
years down the road asking if you'd like to buy into their low-risk,
high-reward investment opportunity

Quite a trip, no? But before you give in to the instant gratification
that can only be brought to you by Amazon, do me a favor and recall
a time when you felt like you really belonged
I know, it must have hard when you were the only one keeping your
parents from divorce,
But I have some advice: stay the course

Way to go, look at you now!
A bright young graduate on the prowl

Don't worry about the six months that have passed since graduation
I'm sure you'll find something to do with that major in art education

A few years pass, and you settle down
At long last, you finally have a kid you can take to the playground

It wasn't long after until you figured out just how difficult marriage can be
Alas, you've never been one to quit prematurely

In the time it took you to drive to the office and back,
Your baby bird is now leaving the nest and seeks wisdom as he packs

A million different quotes enter your head at full force
Until you arrive at the words, "Honey, just stay the course"

Nomad

"Racing down the sideline looks like no one's gonna catch him. Touchdown, Rochester Zebras. A seventy-five-yard reception on the opening play of the game!" the press box announcer exclaimed. Incoherent cheering erupted from the right side of the bleachers while the left side slung dozens of criticisms at their team's coaching staff and players.

"Horrible coverage," "What a bonehead play," and "Who's running the defense?" were just a few of the comments perceivable to the ears of the twenty-two men on the field during the extra-point attempt. These were matched with the student section's own set of cheers.

"BJ Barnes!" followed by five claps to the cadence of dun-dun, dun, dun, dun, echoed throughout the stadium, immediately setting the tone of the game. Of course, our student section also took part in the slander after chanting my name.

"Did the varsity bus break down on the way here?"

"They're all cousins!"

"I don't know what's worse, watching your team lose or the forty-five-minute drive back home."

My teammates slapped me on the back of the helmet and gave me kudos as we jogged over to the forty-yard line for kickoff. It was this play that elevated me from the Texas transfer to captain of the team. I was home. From that play on, I did everything I could on and off the field for the best interest of the team. There was no putting a price on the sounds of the student section chanting my name or the brotherhood that surrounded me at all times. Every game that came was a little sweeter, and that marked one less game left in my high school career. One less opportunity to be a part of a team I was just learning how to succeed on.

The team and I would play our last game on November 1, 2019, and fall to the number one ranked team in the state. I only left the field on account of the lights being switched off. When entering the locker room, the atmosphere had changed remarkably since we had initially left for pregame warm-ups. The towel whipping, underclassmen hazing, and sexual innuendo gesturing had all died off completely. No, this loss was different and not because it meant we were eliminated from state title contention. It meant none of the seniors would ever suit up again for their hometown team. I noticed it was finally starting to set in with them as the look on their faces grew bleaker. The unfathomable truth was upon us. This time, there were no celebratory postgame photo shoots, no interviews for the newspaper, and no optimistic speech telling us "We'll get 'em next week." This time around, Head Coach Sean Kelly was speechless.

"The floor is yours, guys," he said, taking off his baseball cap. In a clockwise rotation, each senior was given the option to say something. Some chose not to say anything at all, others advised the juniors, and so forth. At first, I wasn't going to say much, if anything at all. *A simple "thanks for everything, guys" is the easiest way to go out,* I thought.

That was until I saw junior Jon Kelly, with no relation to the coach, sitting on my right-hand side. He was the first person I had met in my time at Rochester, and I had always pictured him as a little brother. He tapped my foot with his cleats still on and silently mouthed the words, "You've got to say something."

I gave him a subtle nod and thought, *What the hell.* My turn had come.

"Do you want to say anything, BJ?" Coach said, extending the offer in hopes that I would deliver.

Clearing my voice, I responded, "Yeah. I guess I'll start by saying thank you to all the people sitting in this room for giving me a chance. A chance to play football again and for accepting me into this community with open arms. Some of you already know this and some of you don't. For the ones that don't, during my freshman year,

I snapped my forearm in half in a scrimmage the weekend before school started. Not only did this effectively and immediately end my first year of high school football before it even had a chance to start, but I was forced to wear a cast the entire first semester as well. I was then moved to the bottom of the depth chart and forced to write left-handed for eighteen consecutive weeks. I was graded based on my illegible chicken scratch, and the coaches underestimated my abilities all the same. However, if it wasn't for this, I never would have been aware of the teachers' disinterested approach or the cut-throat mentality that is Texas football. They didn't care about me as an individual, and I needed to find somewhere that did. You guys gave me that second chance and, more importantly, somewhere to call home. Thank you." The room sat in silence for a few seconds before Coach Kelly chimed back in.

"If any of you are confused about what a leader looks like, take a look at the young man who just spoke. I was just like you at my age, and it has been my pleasure coaching you, all of you," he said, pointing to the seniors one by one. The locker room gradually thinned out as everyone took off their shoulder pads and jerseys. Amid the commotion, I had gotten sidetracked saying goodbyes and collecting my things; the thought of actually leaving never crossed my mind. I was one of the last ones out when I went to leave, and I couldn't help but to stop and get one last look at the locker room that changed my life. Except, it didn't amaze me the way I imagined it would. The streamers that draped over the varsity bay were ripped apart to shreds, most likely to compensate for the crushed spirits of the senior class. The stereo that played AC/DC until our ears rang was gone. And for some reason I can't explain, the locker room looked dimmer that day. A shadow of what it once was. Its sunken soul was all the evidence I needed to suggest my time had come and gone. As sad as it was, it was time to move on. I had to give up a team and community that was just starting to know my name.

Almost a year later, I moved onto Wherewithal's campus and quickly found myself claustrophobic of my new surroundings. It was during the second week of school I discovered my dorm was classified as a closet through an email sent to me by Wherewithal's Service

Request alias. I spent most of my time there. Three out of four of my classes were remote, and when the weather forbade dining outside, I took my meals back to my closet to eat alone. However, if there was one activity that got me out of my confined quarters, it was football. It was a huge factor for me attending in the first place, so without it, I didn't exactly have an abundance of reasons to get out of bed in the morning. I was the first one to get injured and was out for my first semester of college ball. Go figure. Every practice post-ACL tear involved me standing off to the sideline, watching as my teammates flew around effortlessly. One practice, realizing I had nothing to do, the head coach called me to his side.

"You doing anything?" he asked as he continued to look out onto the field.

"No, sir, I am inactive today, per usual," I said, looking up at him.

"Why don't you come follow me up to the roof above the press box. I wanna show you something," he said, already heading there. After scaling the bleachers, walking through the press box, and climbing up the ladder to the roof, I saw a camera perched on a tripod. "Can you film practice today? We have no one else to film."

"Yes, sir," I responded right away.

"Fantastic. I knew you would step in." I found it a bit odd he was so enthusiastic about pressing a record button on a camera, but that was just his character. He would always say, "Be enthusiastic about everything you do," to the team every week during warm-ups. After giving me the rundown of how to open the aperture and hit record, he expressed why he enjoyed coming up to the roof so often. "You've probably never been up here, have you, Barnes?" he asked as he turned his back to the field and gazed onward toward the horizon.

"No, sir, I have not."

"Helluva view, huh?" he asked, spellbound. I didn't respond. It seemed as if he wouldn't have even heard me if I did. "It's amazing how far you can see from up here. That tree line is probably ten miles away. Every direction leads you somewhere new."

"Uh-huh," I said, nodding. The wind picked up since we had first gotten up there and pushed my unzipped jacket behind me.

"You feel that?" he said. "It's just so freeing being up here. Makes you feel like you're the only man in the world." Lord only knows how much that resonated with me. "Okay, well, I'm going to get back out there, and remember, all you have to do is point and shoot," he said as he made his way back down the ladder. I did just that for the better part of an hour and a half and reflected on what exactly my first semester away from the only home I had ever known boiled down to. Weekdays began to blend together. The grueling repetitive cycle of going to class, injury rehab, class, practice, and then dinner ate me alive.

To combat this, one Friday afternoon before travel restrictions were put into action, it dawned on me that I had no plans for the coming weekend. I rarely did anyway, but I thought, *What is stopping me from going home and catching a game?* While it was a hike, perhaps going home to catch a game on Friday nights would alleviate the isolation and anxiety I was experiencing day in and day out. It was decided. There couldn't possibly be anything worse than the seclusion inside of my dorm. After practice, I took a shower, despite not breaking a sweat, and put on my favorite outfit. A black polo windbreaker, black-and-white-striped Adidas NMDs, black joggers, and a white Rochester Zebras shirt. I never would have believed that in my first semester of college I would look forward to going home more than staying there. It all clicked. This thought alone was the very root to all my frustrations and unhappiness. Wherewithal was not home, and it took every ounce of willpower within me not to fall off a cliff emotionally and academically.

My foot was heavier than normal. One hundred and eighteen miles passed in no time flat as I attempted to sort out the mess that was my first semester. Even so, I had already missed the first half, thanks to practice running late and Indianapolis rush hour traffic. Pulling into a parking spot closest to the entrance, I could hear the sounds coming from the arena.

"And that'll do it for the first half, as Rochester fails to convert," the press box announcer said wearily. The team was 0–5 and struggling to cap their first win of the season. I watched as they marched into the locker room, hanging their heads sorrowfully. I briefly locked eyes with the defensive coordinator, who had praised me time and time again for my efforts on the field the season before. I attempted to say hello, but rather than acknowledging my presence, he shrugged it off and didn't bother saying anything. I was befuddled, to say the least, but I wasn't going to let it ruin my night. I eventually found a seat in the bleachers and watched as the team warmed up. Suddenly, I heard a voice from behind me.

"Yikes. Not a pretty sight." Sure enough, it was my old boss from the television station. He was referring to the scoreboard: 35–0 in favor of the other team.

"Looks like they're not ending the drought tonight," I said, shaking my head and involuntarily chuckling.

"Nope, I don't think so," he said, laughing. "So how have you been?"

"I've been all right," I said, lying through my teeth. "College is great."

"That's good to hear. They really are the best years of your life," he said.

I responded, "Yeah, I bet. I do have to say, though, we aren't allowed to do much of anything."

"Is that so?" he replied. "That's unfortunate. College is about independence and being on your own. That may come with regret and failure, but it's also about finding your true self. I remember my first semester. I never wanted to leave once I got there, and pretty soon, you won't want to come home either."

"Well, enough about me," I said, wanting to change the topic. "How has the TV station been?"

"Busy, but that's how we like it. Speaking of which, I gotta head back up there," he said, turning to the press box. He was filming the game, and the third quarter was minutes away from starting. "It was nice seeing you again, BJ. Take it easy."

"You do the same," I said, as he vanished into the tented press box. The third quarter started, and not much else happened afterward. The opposing team played a conservative run game, dwindling out the clock; likewise, Rochester's predictable run attack only shot them in the foot. As the clock hit triple zeros, the score remained a 35–0 decisive shutout. The regular ambience that surrounded Rochester's gritty hard-nosed mentality had disappeared. The players were drained and the stands, dry. Teams stood on their respective sidelines and waved to each other before heading into the school. Still no photoshoots, no interviews, no gatherings. COVID killed all of it.

I spent the night in a house I once knew as home, but with none of my friends in town or cars to window paint, I felt like I didn't belong there either. I stayed as long as Saturday evening before I couldn't stomach it anymore and regrettably drove back to Sheetzville. While I might have wanted to be anywhere else, there was nowhere for me to go. I still had the responsibility of attending class and practice even if I was only a bystander. I buried my head in work and refused to look up until the semester was over, and sooner or later, it was.

November 20 was here. As I made trips to my car and back, students on all floors were clambering about one another and discussing their plans for next semester.

"I don't know if I can do this again."

"So I'll see you next semester?"

"Time to go home." I noticed the stark contrast between people's responses. There was no middle ground to their opinions. This semester was either the highlight or lowest point in their lives thus far. With one last tote in my hands, I bade farewell to closet 407 and shut the door.

"Is everything out of your dorm, sweetie?" the lady working the front desk said with a scratchy voice and her glasses clinging to the tip of her nose.

Handing in my key, I replied. "Well, I wouldn't really call it a dorm," I said jokingly under my breath.

"What? You're gonna have to speak up, hun," she replied.

"Oh, nothing, nothing. Yes, everything is out of my room."

"Okay, see you next term," she said as I headed for the door. Christmas Day couldn't beat the sensation I was feeling. Leaves crunched under my feet as I made my way back to the car. It was crammed full of everything I managed to fit in my closet, and once

I got in, I never looked back. Sheetzville was a speck in my rearview mirror, a distant memory. My semester shouldn't have unfolded the way it did, and I found it disheartening to be this excited to leave, but I knew I didn't have the strength to go back. Driving down highway US 231, I received a group Facetime call from Bruce and Ray. Still the only two people I'd call my close friends at Wherewithal. Ray left the day before and didn't get an opportunity to say goodbye to Bruce or me.

"Heyyy, boys, what's up," she said, fixing her hair.

"Nothing, just left," Bruce said, looking down at his phone and his hair sticking up.

"How was it?" she asked.

"Good, I couldn't wait to get out of there, honestly," I said with one hand on the wheel.

"Yeah, same," Bruce said.

"Why's that?" she replied, tilting her head the way a dog does when it's confused.

"I can't afford it, Ray," Bruce said in a heavy voice. "I was hoping to get more scholarships, but it just wasn't in the cards. I can never go back." Unsure of what to say back, she asked me the same question.

"Besides being limited to my surroundings, this just wasn't what I was expecting, is all," I said. "It's not even about COVID-19 or my injury, but I just feel like at this time, I've gotten to see Wherewithal for all it's not. Of course, it's not all bad. I found you, but I also lost myself in the process. I can never go through what I just did again."

"No, I get it," she said in a reassuring tone. "I've thought about not returning too. I've decided to come back this next semester, but if things aren't better, then I will transfer." The conversation never recovered after that. We were all in our separate headspaces but felt mutual nevertheless. Once the call ended, I had an hour's worth of driving in front of me. I watched as the tangerine-colored sun began to set over the highway and bounced off the roof of the other cars. The moon had swapped places with the sun by the time I pulled into the driveway of my house in Rochester. My grandmother couldn't hide her euphoria. A normally very stoic woman was shouting from the window with excitement.

"Hurry up and get inside!"

"I'm coming," I said. "Just let me get my things." With a few trips to the car and back, I cleaned out my car.

"I'm so glad you're here," she said.

"I know. I am too," I replied. Her dog, Kona, refused to stop licking my knees.

"Before I get settled in, let me check my email for any announcements my professors might have sent me. I haven't got a chance to check it all day."

"Okay, I'll be out here," she said, sitting in her recliner, watching Fox News. I opened the door to my room, and it was in pristine condition. My grandmother had made the bed and changed the sheets since my last visit. I sat on the edge of my bed and opened my laptop and read my inbox.

"Wherewithal Housing: Thank you for submitting your housing agreement."

"Black Friday Sales: Download the fun."

"Do not reply to this email: You have submitted your assignment for COMM 200."

"Athletic Director Barbra Watts: You have been identified as a close contact." My heart froze as my eyes reread the email over and over. My fingers shook as I clicked on the email.

> Here is the information for the Zoom call tonight.
> You are invited to a Zoom webinar.
> When: Nov 20, 2020 07:00 PM Indiana (East)
> Topic: COVID Intake
> Zoom link below:

I never would have blinked twice at the sight of this same email if I were on campus, but I had just hugged my grandmother five minutes before. It was suspected I had been exposed due to a football-related incident, most likely rehab. I stayed inside my room until the Zoom call was over and then made plans over the phone to stay at Bruce's house for self-quarantine.

"Hey, man, I need to ask a favor. Is it all right if I spend the night? I can't be around my grandma," I said.

"Ooo, does someone have the 'rona?" Bruce asked.

"Dude, stop playing. I need somewhere to stay. Is it all right if I come over?" I asked, thoroughly aggravated.

"Yeah, I don't see why not. Come over whenever," he said. I hung up the phone and packed a go bag as quickly as possible.

"Grandma, I don't really know how to tell you this, but I have to go," I said in the arched frame of the hallway.

"What do you mean? You just got here," she fired right back.

"I've been identified as close contact, and I can't risk being around you." After some heavy contemplation and giving me the death stare, she responded.

"Oh all right, go," she said. She didn't want to let me go, but she also knew neither of us could risk it. I grabbed my keys as we said our goodbyes from a distance and walked out the door.

A short while later, I pulled into Bruce's gravel driveway and met him on his porch.

"Yeah, you can't come inside," Bruce said.

"What do you mean?" I questioned.

"My parents are going to Arkansas for Thanksgiving to visit my sister, and they said they don't want you inside," he said. I interjected immediately.

"But I have nowhere else to go."

"What about Jennifer?" he asked.

"I'm not going to my ex-girlfriend's house. Her mom wouldn't have let me stay the night even when we were together," I barked right back.

"What about Edward?" he proposed once more.

"Out of town," I said.

"Well, I don't know what to tell ya," he said. "You can sleep in the shed."

I replied back with the snarky remark, "Thanks, but I'm going to sleep somewhere I know I can." I moped back to my car, unsure of my next move. With only a go bag and car to my name, suddenly, my closet wasn't looking too bad. I tossed and turned in my seat, turning on my engine for heat every couple of hours. Finally, around 4:00 a.m., I dozed off as snowflakes stuck to my windshield.

I woke up to a thin layer of ice on my windows. My breath was a visible cloud as I flipped the controls to lean my seat forward. I started my car and read 8:06 a.m. on the dashboard. Passing crop fields that began to thaw in the morning sun, I raced to the nearest rapid testing site in the next town over. After a deep nasal swab, the nurse ensured that she would text me my results as soon as they were ready. As tempted as I was to just wait there, several cars were piled up behind me, and I felt disgusting. Even with nowhere to go, I couldn't bear the thought of my appearance. I smelled from the day before, my hair was sticking up, and my lips were chapped blue. I drove over to the Kroger down the road and purchased a bottle of water with the $7.28 remaining in my checking account. I resisted slurping down the whole bottle to save a few ounces to brush my teeth with. Water and toothpaste dripped from the sides of my mouth onto the pavement outside my car door. Gargling and rinsing the toothpaste out of my mouth, I watched as a family passed me by, wondering how I got here. I wondered the same. Closing my car door and awaiting my test results, I sat back in the driver's seat and marveled at the image of me running down the sideline once more.

Greener Pastures

My second semester would start in four days, and I couldn't wrap my head around why a handful of my close friends at Wherewithal willingly chose to move back on campus. The same campus that was quite literally doing itself more harm than good. A campus whose figures in power were more concerned with being politically correct than the happiness of their own students. The campus whose solution to COVID-19 was secluding its students to their dorm rooms for class, meals, and sleep.

Almost every class was remote, and sports were a joke. If one player contracted COVID-19, the entire team would cease practice indefinitely while the athletic department made phone calls contact tracing anyone that person had made eye contact with in the last week. Nevertheless, I digressed because in the beginning, I was convinced that I was the problem. The solution being that if I tried harder to make friends or tried harder to fit the college narrative, I would surely feel at home.

After forcing the hand that was faking it till I fit in ran its course, I tried to crack the burning question as to why I wasn't happy. A question some people never figure out or bothered investigating, for that matter. What was wrong with me? Wherewithal was my dream school, right? It had everything my high school did, and I had a hard enough time parting way with it. Wherewithal offered a small student body, great professors, and most of all, a football team. I was well aware of the trap that run-of-the-mill colleges used to lure in any high school senior who could run with the football. The bait that screamed, "Don't look outside of the lines. Don't research our campus life or the percentage of graduating seniors who are employed within six months." Just worry about putting on that jersey for another four years, and the rest will take care of itself. Although Wherewithal didn't look this way, at least from the outside. Its tight-knit networking chain and alumni spoke for themselves. I thought I just needed to adjust. I wasn't a bookworm, nor was I the life of the party. I wasn't a jock and certainly wasn't an activist. I had always thrived in high school as being the well-rounded social type, but why wasn't it working here?

I was too big, that's why. I had felt claustrophobic at various times throughout the semester, and it wasn't because I was banished to closet 407. Wherewithal was already half the size of its normal capacity by only housing the freshmen and sophomores on campus. Given only a thousand students were there, I had seen every face there was within the first two weeks, but that wasn't all. The small student body gave me a glimpse into the type of students the school was appealing to. Its private label and $67,000 price tag to go alongside was enough to make every spoiled kid in Carmel, Indiana, wet their five-inch inseam golf shorts. This, and they weren't smart enough to make it into any other private school. The ceiling was too short, and my ambition too tall. I was a tuna in a goldfish bowl.

What was frustrating was that Wherewithal hadn't always been this way. I knew of several retired individuals back in Rochester who fell in love with Wherewithal and made a successful career for themselves. Granted they were different times, but I couldn't imagine they'd be pleased by any stretch of the imagination to learn what it had become. They all said some of the best years of their life were spent there. The specialist coach for Rochester, Coach Bashem, had graduated fairly recently, and while he mentioned they were sticklers for money, he couldn't stop himself from telling me stories about his days there in between huddles during practice. Even now, I know a soon-to-be senior from Rochester who attended Wherewithal, and she was single-handedly the nicest person I had ever met. But aside from her, the culture shift that had taken Wherewithal by storm was brewing a toxic environment I wanted no part in.

The only thing holding me back was the game I fell in love with. The game that was unforgiving while also being the most rewarding. How could I say goodbye to football when I felt like I was just reaching my potential? Easy, when it was the only thing standing in the way of me being truly happy. And while that might sound like an overstatement, every school I thought I had a chance at playing at looked all too familiar. Division III, private, and small. I was not going D1, Bama wasn't standing by, and there was no point in transferring if it meant my situation wouldn't improve. I needed scenery drastically different than Wherewithal, and if that meant checking off every box Wherewithal couldn't while only leaving the one next to football blank, that was a reality I was going to have to accept. As was with most things, sacrifice was X in the problem that stumped me the duration of my first semester at college. If I wanted to rush, stay out till three, and discover my calling while not feeling like I was out of my element, transferring to a large recognizable school in a place I had never been was the answer.

The transfer process wasn't easy. It was not often talked about, and it was not advertised, but in some cases, it was necessary. The school I once knew and fell in love with during the admissions process wasn't the same university I know today, and that was okay. Initially, I thought I was alone, but I knew of an abundance of other students who had decided to transfer as well. At first, I wanted to save the school I thought was for me until I realized that they didn't want to be. I wasn't going to compromise my abilities or passion just to walk in line to the predetermined, mediocre beat of someone else's drum. My school wasn't gold; it was tarnished.

I had witnessed firsthand how my peers struggled with college, COVID, and life transitions. The mixture of all three created an inimical concoction that skewed their judgment and manifested self-doubt. I had watched hometown heroes drink themselves into depression. I had seen Miss Teen Illinois question her beauty after getting turned down by every sorority. I was there when my closest friend decided to drop out after believing he didn't have what it took to make it at college. I myself had wondered if I truly belonged anywhere, but if there was one thing I was sure of, it was that we'd all be fine by fall.

Not Another Teen Playlist

This playlist is a combination of songs that in essence, follow the same life lessons I mention throughout the book in the same order as they appear. While one option is to use it as a soundtrack as you read along, I highly suggest listening to it after you've read the book in order to double down on the lyrics in hopes they resonate with you as they did for me. Sharing a similar approach as the book it finds itself in, this playlist was formed over the span of many months in hopes that it could heal or at least relieve the scars shared by so many in these surreal times.

1. The Show Must Go On - Queen
2. Old Days - Chicago
3. September - Earth, Wind & Fire
4. See You Again - Tyler, The Creator
5. Free Bird - Lynyrd Skynyrd
6. California Dreamin' - The Mamas & The Papas
7. Viva la Vida - Coldplay
8. All By Myself - Eric Carmen
9. 1979 - The Smashing Pumpkins
10. Take Me Back to Chicago - Chicago
11. Prom Night - Chance the Rapper
12. My Generation - The Who
13. Young Dumb & Broke - Khalid
14. Daydream Believer - The Monkees
15. Mary Jane's Last Dance - Tom Petty & The Heartbreakers
16. Love Is Like Oxygen - The Sweet
17. 911/ Mr. Lonely - Tyler, the Creator
18. FEEL. - Kendrick Lamar

19. Pursuit of Happiness - Kid Cudi
20. Telephone Line - ELO
21. O-o-h Child - The Five Stairsteps
22. It's Not Unusual - Tom Jones
23. Jack & Diane - John Cougar
24. Who Wants to Live Forever - Queen
25. Landslide - Fleetwood Mac
26. History - 88rising
27. Daisy Jane - America
28. The Things We Do for Love - 10cc
29. Circles - Post Malone
30. Someone Saved My Life Tonight - Elton John
31. It's a Beautiful Day - Michael Buble
32. Made For You - Jake Owen
33. Lonely Boy - Andrew Gold
34. Small Town - John Mellencamp
35. Stairway to Heaven - Led Zeppelin
36. Yesterday - The Beatles
37. The Air That I Breathe - The Hollies
38. Graduation - benny blanco & Juice WRLD
39. She - Harry Styles
40. Hotel California - Eagles
41. Lights - Journey
42. Our Town - James Taylor
43. Home Sweet Home - Motley Cru
44. Goodbye Yellow Brick Road - Elton John
45. Ghost Town - Kanye West
46. Crazy - Gnarls Barkley
47. I Ran (So Far Away) - A Flock of Seagulls
48. Everybody Wants to Rule the World - Tears for Fears
49. Reelin' In the Years - Steely Dan
50. Heroes - David Bowie

About the Author

B.J. Barnes was your typical high school senior—captain of the football team, president of his school's volunteer organization, and member of the National Honors Society. He, as well as the rest of his tight-knit class, knew the glory days had to end at some point; only nothing could have prevented his youth's untimely demise. He would spend the next few months working toward a diploma from home. No prom. No senior prank. No final curtain call. Although he did have college to look forward to, right? After graduating from his quaint high school in the boondocks of Northern Indiana, he was fortunate enough to be accepted into a private university about two and a half hours south. There, he had the opportunity to rush, meet new people, and work toward a degree all from the comfort of his sixty-four-square-foot dorm room. Only one small problem: he was rarely allowed to be anywhere else.

I invite you to join him in his debut nonfictional book, *COVID, College, & Life Transitions*, in which he discusses firsthand the angst, fear, loneliness, and independence that comes with transitioning from being a high school senior to a modern-day college student amid a global pandemic.